A Taste of the
AEGEAN

PAVILION

A Taste of the
AEGEAN
Greek Cooking and Culture

By ANDY HARRIS *with*
photographs by TERRY HARRIS

To our parents, Alec and Jeanne, who first
had the courage to drive us to Greece

Acknowledgements
Thanks to Colin Webb for the commission, Joanne Rippin for
her patience as an editor, Pamela Todd for her constant faith as
an agent, Kodak, Thomson Holidays and everyone in Greece
who welcomed us into their homes.

Previous pages: *Picking olives in
autumn*.

First published in Great Britain in 1992 by
PAVILION BOOKS LIMITED
London House, Great Eastern Wharf,
Parkgate Road, London SW11 4NQ
This edition published in 1999

Text copyright © Andy Harris 1992, 1999
Photographs copyright © Terry Harris 1992, 1999

Designed by Lee Griffiths

A CIP catalogue record for this book is
available from the British Library.

ISBN 1 85145 941 3

10 9 8 7 6 5 4 3 2

Printed and bound by Kyodo Printing Co (Singapore) Ltd

Contents

PREFACE 7

THE ISLAND 9
  Dolmadakia 32
  Militinia 32
  Easter Salad 34
  Summer Salad 34
  Kolokythia Gemista Me Avgolemono 34
  Moustalevria 35
  Sfougato 35
  Skordalia 35

FISHING IN THE AEGEAN 37
  Arni Sto Fourno Me Patates 42
  Arni Fricassée 42
  Meitzanosalata 42
  Octapodi Me Kremithia 43
  Bakaliaros Yiachni 43
  Sardelles Sto Fourno 44
  Kakavia 44
  Soupies Me Spanaki 44
  Fassoulada 45

OTHER ISLANDS IN THE SUN 47
  Avgolemono 80
  Faki 80
  Fava 80
  Mayeritsa 82

  Skaltsounia 82
  Domates Gemistes 83
  Gemista 83
  Kokkina Avga 84
  Revitho-Keftedes 84
  Lagos Stifado 84

MOUNTAINS, LAKES AND PLAINS 87
  Autumn Salad 126
  Spanakorizzo 126
  Hirino Me Prassa 126
  Soutzoukakia 128
  Briam 128
  Spetsofai 129

THE CITY 131
  Anginares Me Koukia 144
  Garides Giouvetsi 144
  Pasteli 146
  Melitzanes Sto Fourno 146
  Vissinada 146
  Saganaki 147
  Yiouvarlakia 147

GLOSSARY 150

INDEX 151

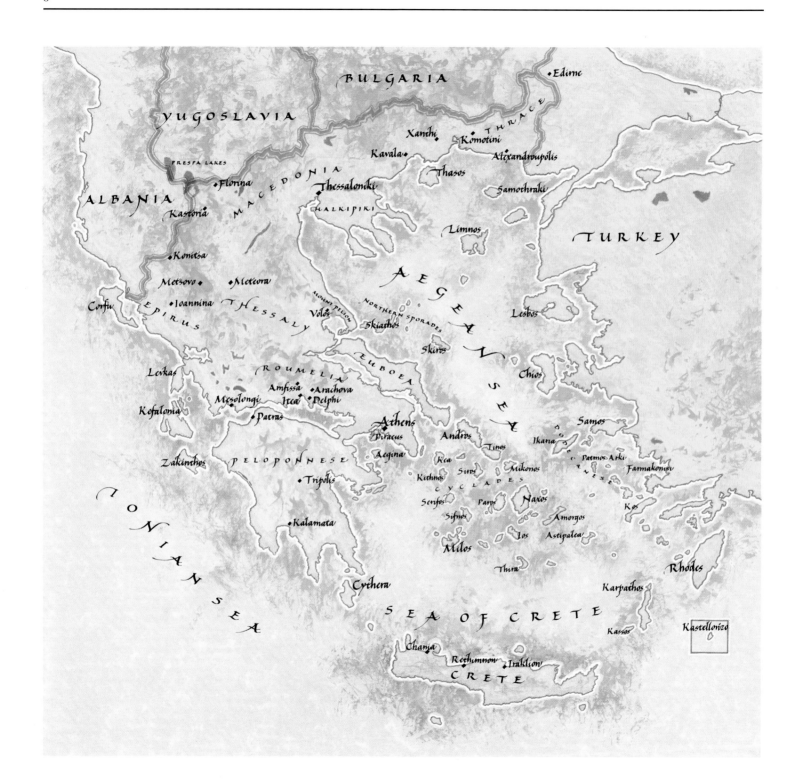

Preface

This is not merely a cookery book full of recipes, it is also an exploration into the ways in which the Greeks live and eat. Under attack by adapted European and American habits, the ethics of the nouveau riche classes in the cities and the return of exiles from abroad with their disdain for all things that belong to the past, this mediterranean nation is in a state of constant, irrevocable change. Perhaps because Greece is one of the last mediterranean countries to develop, its cuisine remains untouched. There is no battle between rival chefs fighting the Michelin star wars with guileful adaptations of old recipes, but there are plenty of cooks who continue to make dishes in exactly the same way as their ancestors. This book is not an elegy as it is too late for that now that tourism has established its rags-to-riches hold. But it is a celebration of what remains – a continuity of inheritance that shows that life still must go on.

The influence of the Ottoman Empire is indelibly stamped on Greece's culinary subconscious in the sophistication of Middle-Eastern sweets, the use of spices, like cumin in meat dishes, and the widespread practice of stuffing vegetables and making savoury pastries. Many claim that the basis of present-day Greek cuisine is wholly influenced by this sophistication and the influx of refugees from Asia Minor in 1922. This is partly true on the mainland and on the larger islands like Crete and Rhodes but, in the traditional cooking methods of the smaller islands of the Aegean and areas like the Mani not subjected to Turkish rule, there is a cuisine more directly linked to an ancient past.

The ancient Greeks were probably even more sophisticated than the Turks and eating and drinking was a recognized art-form with Greek chefs and pastry-makers much in demand in the fashion conscious Roman Empire. Food theorists and historians like Archestratus, Theophrastus and Athenaeus provide documented accounts of these obsessions. Athenaeus in his laborious and learned *Deipnosophistae* (or *Sophists at Dinner*) shows how they would discuss the merits of tuna belly from Byzantium or truffles from Mytilini and the various ways of cooking them. Something of that obsession survives today in the way the season's new fruit and vegetables are awaited and the excitement that every Greek experiences as they crowd around caiques to see what has been caught. Rooted in the seasons, cuisine plays a basic, never-ending role to the rhythms of everyday Greek life.

The Island

Ios, Sikinos, Serifos, Milos
'Each word a swallow
to bring you spring in the midst
    of summer' he said
And ample the olive groves
To sift the light through their fingers
that it may spread gently over
    your sleep
and ample the cicadas
which you will feel no more
than you feel the pulse inside
    your wrist
but scarce the water
so that you hold it a god and understand the
    meaning of its voice
and the tree alone
no flock beneath it
so that you take it for a friend
and know its precious name
sparse the earth beneath your feet
so that you have no room to spread your roots
and keep reaching down in depth
and broad the sky above
so that you read the infinite on your own
THIS WORLD
this small world the great!
                    Odysseus Elytis from *The Axion Esti*

Above: *The classic symbol of the Greek Kafeneon.* Left: *A Cycladic island in spring.*

It is early July and another day of perfect calm on an island beseiged by a windless, indigo sea. The voices of the village are quiet but the sounds that pervade the night air begin before dawn with the braying of donkeys and mules, an occasional owl's hoot and the last rattling screech of the bats. In this village it is said that the anguished call of a donkey on the terraces below is a triumphant wheeze of ecstacy for the lucky one who has found the rare ass or she-donkey. Probably their cries sense another day of toil and sweat.

Those people that go to the fields, men of all ages and some daughters, wake just before dawn with the echoing sound of cockcrow. Those that remain, wives and grandmothers, start the day with sweeping rituals and the noise of radios playing melancholic island songs. Kitchens and front rooms are swept of any dust and breadcrumbs from the night before and rag carpets are aired in the brightening sun.

The first bus leaves at 7am for the port Alo Pronia, and drops men along the road near paths

Dimitris the fisherman and his children proudly showing a newly caught rophos *(grouper).*

are unbearable in the deep heat of summer. Only determined tourists brave the beach in the afternoon; everyone else attempts fitful siestas at home.

There are two shops, a basement restaurant in the backstreet hotel and an *ouzerie*, a small room with a few chairs and tables outside, that serves *mezedes*. If ouzo is ordered, a few raw *kochilia* (snails), *petalides* (limpets) or *tsiros* (dried fish) appear with slices of cucumber. The tourists are offered *souvlaki*, bacon and eggs, chips and salad.

There is also one *kafeneon* (coffee house) that has been there longer than any other and serves as a meeting place for the islanders. Here, the *mezedes* are very popular – big plates of chopped sausages and bacon, olives, tomatoes and thin chips. In the summer, the islanders sit inside after the nets have been cleaned and prepared to be put out in the evening. The talk is mostly about the day's catch. Every year the fishing deteriorates for there are too many families in the summer, freezing the catch to take back to Athens for the winter months. There are also too many novices fishing in the same place every day with no accumulated knowledge of the sea. Not that the commercial fishermen, with crew to pay and children to support, are up in arms about the situation. At least there are no foreign trawlers using sophisticated radar or long-haul seign nets to make a mockery of the basic techniques still used by most caiques in the Aegean.

It is hard for them to go further away because they then meet the caiques of other islands. Besides, commercial fishing came late to the island. There is no tradition, as with the sponge fishermen of Dodecanese islands like Kalymnos or Symi, of travelling for months in search of good fishing grounds. Here, the caique is not home. One of the fishermen, Dimitris (who used to be a shepherd), frequently speeds out of the port for five minutes, lays his nets within sight of the quay, and is back to drink his ouzo left on the table. Nothing in this modern port is very Greek

that lead to their animals and terraced fields. It stops in front of the old spring, now hidden by a canary-yellow post-box, and the driver jumps out to inspect his tyres. The harbour is empty, everyone is out collecting their nets laid the night before.

A rash of cement houses mushroom on both sides of the bay. One hundred years ago, there were five stone buildings, now in ruins, and little else. But today an ugly wave of cheap, summer housing pock-marks a beach of pebbles and some pumice stone, a reminder of nearby Santorini's last volcanic explosion in 1956. The beach, and the houses made of sweating cement, except the chance to eat some fresh fish and the habit of sitting around watching the foreigners. While drinking *frappé* – shaken and frothy glasses of cold Nescafé – the *xeni* (foreigners) can be seen struggling with their anchors and ropes, babies and lilos.

There is a new quay which has irrevocably changed the island. Where once the ferries were met, whatever the weather, by two small rowing boats and possessions precariously handed down, now they can dock and unload cars and goods for the shops in a matter of minutes.

Anything is possible these days and there is a second wave of expansion happening here. The old mule-trains that carried everything up to the village have been replaced by vans and lorries from other islands bringing building materials. New, perhaps better, tavernas and shops will be built along the rocky road being hewn out of the cliff-face on either side of the port.

With the arrival of the new quay came the modern gypsy caravan consisting of lorries, trucks and vans. These *tsigani* (or *gyfti*) travel from island to island and from city suburb to town square, selling their wares with the aid of a loudspeaker.

The first gypsy van to ever arrive on the island was greeted with great suspicion. It sold an assortment of tablecloths, sheets, blankets and napkins to a few adventurous islanders. Stopping between the two villages, a megaphone announced with monotonous regularity their wares in broken Greek, as the children knocked at every household door. The response was limited but this smart gypsy did not give up and after talking to villagers to see what they needed, returned with a van full of fruit and vegetables.

Another gypsy family came in a lorry selling fowl. The megaphone bellowed, 'come and get some beautiful lively chicks, come and take them away, beautiful chicks.' On this lorry, a misspelt sign offers *fassiano* (pheasant), *perdika* (partridge), *ortika* (quail), *galo* (turkey), *papies* (duck), *kotopoulo* (chicken) and *poulakia* (chicks) an exotic selection treated with disdain.

On a thick blanket beside the lorry the gypsy couple's baby is surrounded by some of the islanders. The other gypsy children climb like spiders over the blankets and carpets tied to the roof of the lorry. The feathers from the caged birds are chased up the street by the four dogs of the island as the gypsy family prepare to catch the ferry to the next island.

Compared to the real village on the mountain top, the port is a lazy place for Greek and foreign holiday-makers alike. In the winter, it is a sad and empty husk of boarded up houses with peeling paintwork. A few builders continue work on new houses but most have returned to the

Gypsy lorry selling live poultry to the islanders.

safe, secure world of the family home up the hill.

The journey between the two villages making up the small capital of the island, takes barely five minutes but the two are wholly different in character. Castro, the lower village, is home to the main church in the subdued Venetian square, the kafeneons and shops. The near-deserted top village of Chorio, however, has slowly been abandoned over the years. The eleven families that remain are fiercely independent and proud of Chorio, even if it is in desperate need of repair. There are ruined houses in every narrow street and gaping holes in roofs are covered by the prolific branches of jasmine. A rogue fig tree takes root in the corner of an old fireplace, shade for the lithe cats that have established a pirate-hold with their threatening, demagogic miaows and squabbling in kitchen courtyards.

Around all this decay, the families continually weed and whitewash their stretches of street and courtyard not with obsessive cleanliness like tourist Mykonos, proud of its title as 'tidiest village in the Aegean', but as a working place where the home is the traditional showcase of Greek hospitality, each one a microcosm of the village unit.

Outside, the streets belong to the donkeys and weeds, worn paving stones fighting against the crumbling rubble of fallen masonry. Shaded from the sun, the narrow streets eventually become the rocky paths leading to the ancient

Right: *The village square and church, focus for most island celebrations.*

*Scraping thyme-scented honey
from the bee-hives.*

*Right: Sun-dried figs and onions
ready for winter storage.*

that it owes its unique and pure flavour.

The donkeys and mules, for which the island is also famous (Herodotus mentions them in his Histories), often stumble along the way to guttural commands of 'Ute!', 'Whe'ist!', 'Na Mula!' ('Come on mule!') and frequent 'Tsk, tsk!' sounds, for which every area has its own harmonic variations on the same theme. Some of the donkeys have names, especially the lazy or cunning ones. This is an enclosed society where humans and animals are given nicknames as soon as they can make it into the fields.

Adonis, the shop-owner is called 'Monacos' (lonely one) after a particularly uneventful childhood; the retired mule-man Yannis, once a familiar daily sight leading his bread-train down to the port with fresh loaves, is called 'Petaktaris' (restless one) and his brother Dimitris, with his arthritic hobble, is called 'Y Arkouda' (the bear) because of his staggered dancing style like a circus bear on a rope.

The donkeys are inextricably tied to island life, for without them the terraces could not be reached, and their passion for *agathi* (thistles) is often tolerated along the route. They are always stopping, grabbing at any chance to eat their favourite *gaidouragatho* (donkey's thistles) the blue eryngo plant whose hard, round heart can also be eaten raw.

On their way to the terraces, the men will sometimes stop by an almond tree to collect handfuls of *amygdala* and, earlier in May, *tsagala* the young green almonds that can be eaten whole. Now, in early July, the *syka* (figs) on the many trees across the island are still small and unripe, only fit for using in *glyka tou koutaliou*, the sweet spoon-preserves always offered to a guest in a Greek home. Later in the year, when they are ripe, they will be collected and eaten fresh or left to dry in the fields or on roofs. Some are kept for the animals, others are roasted with sesame seeds in the oven. The heat kills any worms inside the figs and they are then stored to eat in the winter months or sent to relatives in Athens.

terraces and cliffs around the island.

Before the sun rises, the donkeys take the men along these frequently steep and winding myriad paths to their fields far away. Beside them, spindly fennel plants go to seed and on the neglected terraces and inclines wild *thymari* (thyme) bushes are in purple flower.

It is these fragrant bushes that give such a special flavour (and expensive price) to the island's *meli* (honey). Together with the equally barren island of Anafi further south, the island's *meli* is thought of as being among the finest in Greece. The complete absence of pine trees and the very small production by a few families assures its high price. But it is to the prolific wild thyme, and a few other aromatic plants,

On the island, June is still called *Theristis* and July *Alonaris* after the seasonal traditions of harvesting and threshing of wheat. Similarly, September is known as *Trigitis* after 'Trigos', the grape harvest. People still say, 'Pao sto theros' ('I'm going to harvest'), or, 'Pao sto Trigos' ('I'm going to the grape-picking') if met on the mule tracks to the fields.

Fifteen years ago, the *sitari* (wheat) was still harvested and taken to the one remaining mill. Every family would then make their own large round loaves, from both wheat and barley, and bake them in the village oven. Now, though, they buy bread from the bakers and harvest *vromi* (oats) and *krithari* (barley) for animal feed. Some wheat is still grown for its seeds and to make *kolyva*, the memorial wheat dish made from boiled kernels, nuts, herbs, pomegranate seeds and sugar.

The early summer crops of green peppers

An islander oversees the flour milling inside the windmill.

and tomatoes are growing larger all the time and *ambelofasoula* (early green beans) are ready to be picked. Makeshift scarecrows made out of bamboo, plastic bags and old clothes are erected near the *alonia* (threshing floors) and in the fields. One imaginative farmer is using the phallic sculptures painted in gaudy Pop Art colours, abandoned by an English artist who once lived here, to keep the hooded crows away from his crops.

The last of the *skorda* (garlic) and *kremithakia* (onions) are always picked at this time of year to make way for another later crop of beans.

The early green beans are boiled and eaten with olive oil, vinegar and *skordalia* (garlic sauce) as an evening meal with some local goat's cheese. There are also the first *peponia*, the hairy striped melon that is either eaten now as a crisp cucumber cut into quarters or later, when it ripens as the melon that it really is.

Apart from the wheat and olive trees, the other main crop that has been cultivated without fail since ancient times is the vine. There are terraces on high cliffs overlooking the sea where thick, knotted branches are left untended and seem to tumble like green waterfalls into the waves. These are the wild vines long forgotten or too far away to bother about. Now the grapes are beginning to tighten into small bunches and, on those vines that are closer to hand, they are inspected every other day. In late August or September, the grape-picking begins and the donkeys have an even harder time with the horse-flies, wasps and hornets covering the overfilled baskets tied either side of their crude wooden saddles. The *retsina* made by every family in late September is an unadulterated, heavily resinated wine that, with some re-education of the palate, is perfectly drinkable, especially if chilled. This is wine made using the same methods as the ancient Greeks, only barrels are used today instead of amphora to store the wine.

Every family has a *kellari* (outside storeroom) with a stone trough in which to tread the grapes.

The ancient methods of wine-making are still widely used on the islands, here the grapes are picked from the terraced vines close to the sea.

Treading the grapes in stone kellaria.

Here the barrels are made ready to store the new wine.

A small hole leads to a lower square trough that holds the grape-juice and the spiky barbs of some brushwood act as an effective filter between the two. The treading is done over several days, often in cramped conditions, for many of the *kellaria* are more like caves. Ropes are tied to the twisted olive trunk beams to hold on to and after many hours the men emerge, stung by the wasps and covered in the purple flush of treading, to drink the *mousto* (unfermented grape-juice). Later, one of the favourite Greek desserts is made, *moustalevria*, a jelly-like mix of the boiled grape-juice mixed with flour, sesame seeds and cinnamon dusted on top.

The wine is put into small barrels and is ready to drink after 40 to 45 days but most of it is kept for drinking in the cold winter months. By the following July or August, many people have finished their supplies or the wine has turned to vinegar. Foreigners often think it tastes like it anyway and the villagers call the last few bottles 'Dynamite' after the effect it has on their stomachs.

Three types of wine are made. First, there is *retsina*, which takes its name from the *retsini* (pine-resin) that is always added. Then there is *kokkineli*, a light red wine made with a mixture of red and white grapes and resin, and finally there is *yialisto*, a dark, sweet wine. No resin is added to this wine as the grapes used for it are shrivelled for about ten days in the sun, like a French *Vin de Paille*, to create a concentrated flavour.

There are eight grape varieties grown on this island, all known by their local names, *Monemvasia* and *Mandilaria* are the most widely cultivated, but *Tsagarines*, *Smyrneika*, *Tsordo-Sidika*, *Nikita*, *Rosaki* and *Fraoula*, a strawberry-coloured grape, are also grown. As of old, all are mixed indiscriminately and considered to be a basic point of departure to which only resin is added. Half a kilo of resin is added to every one hundred kilos of *mousto*, a high proportion for this chemical-free wine. Centuries ago the ancient Greeks would also have added sea-

Collected kindling and straw is taken to the bakery to use as starter fuel for firing the oven for the early morning loaves.

Far right: *One of the villagers with her freshly baked Easter biscuits*

water, honey, flowers and herbs.

Those who work close to the village return for lunch. Then, there is a stillness on the terraces again that mourns the earlier Cycladic era. The agricultural process has changed little since then and when hoeing the same fields today, sometimes a fragment of a white marble figure covered in the same thick crust of red clay turns up. These are the Cycladic figures that influenced Picasso, Brancusi, Moore and Modigliani. They remain enigmatic figures of worship, as difficult to understand as the powerful Easter Island statues.

Each family has plots of land scattered around the island, all planted with different basic crops. Some lie fallow for one year or untended because their dry stone walls are beyond repair. Once – and ruined farmhouses around the island testify to this – a family would spend weeks away from the village when the olive harvest was in progress. But now most of the island is left to the destructive wind and rain, and the winding and narrow mule paths that snake towards the terraces on the steep cliffs have become overgrown with spiky bushes and precarious with fallen stones. There is no longer the population to support these inaccessible fields

and, besides, why should they bother when PASOK, the popular socialist party in Greece, sends its local minister over with good news? 'Stop being farmers, there's no future in it. Turn to tourism and we can give you small business grants to open bars, change your kellaria into guest houses', he promised in the June 1989 elections.

In Castro, there are two *kafeneia*, two general shops that sell everything but frequently have nothing fresh worth buying to eat, a butcher and a baker. They all open at 8am and in the *kafeneon*, old men too crippled or lazy to go to the fields anymore eke out their meagre pensions all day long. They begin with sweet cups of *metrio*, thick coffee served in *flitzanakia*, white, solid-handled cups. There is also one good-natured drunk who starts as he means to go on with a glass of ouzo.

Perhaps it is Yourgos the baker who works hardest of all, day in day out, collecting brushwood from the hills for his oven. He is almost always covered in flour or soaked in sweat as he works the fire, scraping the embers into an earthenware amphora at least three times a day, except Sundays. *Stakti* (embers) was used throughout Greece to whiten washed clothes

Kolatsio, a working lunch of bread, cheese, sweet red onions and parsley ready to be taken to the fields.

Oven tools and battered metal tins of Easter lamb and potatoes ready for roasting.

and it is still used to clear grape-juice when making *moustalevria* or *petimezi*, the sweet, unfermented grape-syrup.

This is a village where it is unthinkable to be without the daily loaf of fresh, crusty bread. There is no need to make anything else, except the double-baked *paximadia* (dried bread rusks with anise or cumin seeds) found in every household. It is used as a standby when the loaf runs out, sometimes softened in a glass of fresh goat's milk and always taken to the fields for a *kolatsio* (mid-morning snack) with some cheese, wine and raw onion or garlic.

Yourgos, thick-set with a friendly grin, has no time for any of the *stafidopsomo* (raisin bread), *eliopsomo* (olive bread) or *tiropittes* (cheese pies) found in many enterprising bakeries elsewhere. The first batch of about 50 loaves comes out at 10am and they are dusted and covered with lengths of faded cloth to await the eager customers. There will often be tapsia, round, thin aluminium baking tins used for dishes like *domates ke piperies gemistes* (stuffed tomatoes and peppers) or *kreas sto fourno me patates* (roast lamb or goat with potatoes) which the villagers bring to be cooked during the day. Sometimes there is also a sad-looking chicken

with *kritharaki* (an oval rice-shaped pasta) or *hilopittes* (broken curly-shaped egg noodles) that are universally used in Greek cooking to absorb all the cooking juices in roasts and stews.

From mid-July until the end of August, because of the island's increased population, there never seems to be enough bread for the families and friends that return to open their summer houses by the sea. The only extra work Yourgos dare not refuse is to make the church bread (*prosforo*) with a religious stamp on it. He bakes these loaves every Saturday for Sunday's service or whenever there is a mass that it is ordered for. He also bakes *Christopsomo*, with a cross on it, for all the village to consume on Christmas Day; *laganes*, unleavened and oval-shaped with sesame seeds for *Kathari Deftera* (Clean Monday) forty days before Easter in the first week of Lent, and *lazaropsomo* with currants and sesame seeds, for the Saturday before Easter in the sixth week of Lent.

The largest shop in the village is called *To Pefko* (after the stunted pine tree outside) and belongs to an elderly couple, Adonis and Abelia. They are both stricken by arthritis but alert as ever to a new customer who might be sold an idle bottle of whisky, unbelievably cheaper than it is in many places in Scotland. The bottles of Johnny Walker Red Label sit in a corner of the shop covered in dust, waiting to be grabbed by some tourist prospectors. After the incredible journey by lorry, boat and donkey the bottles rest among the tins of *Nov Nov* (the favourite condensed milk in Greece), plastic shoes, mammoth bras and beeswax church candles. Poor Johnny Walker looks down from the label with his cane and top hat, the very image of the proper gentleman, smiling at the folly of his final resting place.

Depending on the day of the week, there is a mad scramble to be first in the shop to buy the few fresh vegetables that the ferry has brought. Wednesday is usually *I mera yia lahanika* the day for vegetables when a few wooden boxes of large tomatoes, shiny aubergines (eggplants), misshapen green peppers and fat courgettes (zucchini) (ideal for making *kolokythia gemista me avgolemeno*), are barely opened before the rationing begins.

Regulars like the priest's wife, who has a large and hungry family to feed; favourites like the mayor's wife; recent widows like Kyria Eleni; foreigners like the doctor, schoolteacher and policeman, need never rush into the shop. Money will not buy even a kilo of tomatoes if one's name is not on that unwritten list.

The other village shop is run by one of the daughters of one-armed Christo, a permanent reminder of an early fishing accident with dynamite that is a familiar occurrence on Greek islands. The rivalry between the two shops can be intense. 'I'm selling my Sprite and Fanta cans at 65 drachmae, that's 20 less,' Adonis reminds his customers without actually ever mentioning the other shop. 'See how much better our tomatoes are and we have peaches!' says the wily daughter.

The butcher sits outside with Rico, his very black cat. Once a shepherd always a shepherd and Yani has returned to the island to open the empty but beautiful butcher's shop. After selling his flock ten years ago to join his brother as a lorry driver in Athens, on the road to untold trucker's wealth, he is a perfect example of the city exodus back to the island and mountain villages of rural Greece.

Forty years ago, during the ravages of starvation and poverty brought on by the confusions of civil and world war, the Greeks, like most of the impoverished southern countries in the Mediterranean, began to leave the homeland for the New World, especially Australia, Canada and the United States, Brazil and South Africa. Now they are back into island life with a vengeance.

Yani keeps enough frozen *brizoles* to satisfy the craving for pork chops, looks after a few goats and sheep again and tends his fields. But he is happiest when whittling away at another shepherd's crook and is found on most days in the nearby *kafeneon* waiting for customers to

Interior of the butcher's shop with its typical three-legged chopping block.

Yani the butcher with his animal hides curing in a deserted house.

Kyria Katina and her husband carrying food back from the baker's oven, wrapped in cloth to keep the flies away.

buy one of his French frozen chickens.

Inside, the shop is a still-life just waiting to be painted by a colourist like RF Kitaj. Two chopping blocks, painted white, hobble on three legs. Behind them, two metallic peacocks that belong in an Indian shanty-town, are nailed to the wall painted in the favourite pale blue of the island. Two tattered photographs, one of a caique and the other of a cow, hint at the dual role of the shop as unofficial fishmonger as well as official butcher. Next to the French chickens and the peas, there is a freezer compartment filled with packets of frozen octopus from Taiwan.

Everything, including the owner, idles all day long. The exception is Easter, when Yani wields his knife like a crazed conductor with his baton. This is the only time that the lethargy breaks and he slaughters lean *katsikia* (goats) and *arnia* (sheep) for all the village. He is paid for this service with the hides which are scraped, dried and hung from the beams in a deserted house at the end of the village. They fetch a good price in the Monastiraki flea market in Athens where they are converted into tourist leather goods.

July is a time for whitewashing houses and *vasilikos* (basil) plants are given a predominant place near doorways once again to help keep flies away from rooms. Any visitor to a house will always brush a hand over the basil leaves or pick the white flowers to release its strong, peppery aroma.

School has finished until September and the 11am bus is filled with mothers and children who go down to the beach for a few hours. At 1pm, they all rush back to the village for lunch and siestas. In the evenings, the children will be helping their fathers with the family chores. The donkeys need to be watered, fed and put into the fields; or they may be sent down to the shops to buy some *fasolia gigantes* (giant white beans) to soak overnight for tomorrow's meal.

With the exception of the Easter festivities, the daily meals are hardly every planned. Rather, they are put together in a direct response to what is coming in from the fields. If there is

nothing at a particular time, the shops are resorted to for dried pasta; lentils for *fakes* soup; split peas for *fava*; tins of the excellent Greek tomato paste and tomatoes for sauces; salted anchovies taken from large tins; imported Irish or Dutch Greek-style cheeses; Naxos *graviera* cheese; tins of Portuguese sardines and mackerel fillets. Then there is always the omnipresent Zwan, a Dutch luncheon meat found inevitably in every Greek store.

Bakaliaros (salt cod) imported from Iceland is another standby product for the winter months. It is almost as popular in Greece as it is in Portugal though there are definitely fewer versions than that country's reputed different recipe for every day of the year. The favourite way of cooking it is *tiganitos me skordalia*, fried with garlic sauce, or *plaki*, baked with tomatoes and onions.

Potatoes make up a very large part of the diet and are usually present at every meal. Chips are easily prepared and fried in olive oil, usually in a *saganaki*, the two-handled pan that gives its name to any kind of fried or baked cheese. Excellent waxy potatoes, known as *axiotikes*, after the island of Naxos where they are grown, are also sometimes boiled and made into a salad with tomatoes, onions and capers.

Eggs are also eaten unashamedly almost every day; fried, or in omelettes with potatoes or courgettes or scrambled with tomatoes. The last is a favourite lunchtime dish found all over Greece in varying forms. It is universally known as *sfougato* (which comes from the word for sponge), *strapatso* or *strapatsada* (both words mean damaged) or simply as *avga me domates* (eggs and tomatoes). In the Peloponnese, it is cooked with spring onions and parsley as *kayiani*, and in Thrace it appears in Muslim villages with green peppers and tomatoes, a combination that comes from Turkey where it is called *menemen*.

Avga me domates is one of those easy dishes to prepare. With the right ingredients, like over-ripe, sugary tomatoes and green olive oil, it

Every island home has a summer basil pot on a windowsill.

five, Kyria Katina makes the two-hour journey to milk the flock near the tumbledown *kellari* used to make and store the cheese.

There are three types of strong goat's cheese: *tiri*, *mizithra* and *tsinogolo*. *Tiri* and *tsinogolo* ('Tsino' means sour) are made with fresh milk, *mizithra* with boiled milk. *Tiri* and *mizithra* are moulded varieties of hard curd cheese, whereas *tsinogolo*, as its name suggests, is a soft curd cheese mixed with salt which tastes a little like sour cottage cheese.

For *tiri*, Kyria Katina pours the milk into a large *kasani* (metal urn) and adds a small amount of commercial *pita* (rennet). After about one and a half hours, when the milk curdles, she uses a special wooden stick called a *taraktis* to stir and then collect the solidified cheese. The cheeses are placed in bamboo baskets, *tirovolia*, covered with muslin and left to drain. By evening they are ready to be placed in tins of *almira* (salted water) where they are left for a minimum of four days.

Mizithra is made by boiling the milk in the *kasani* over a wood fire until the curds suddenly coagulate. Then they are moulded with salt and left on *kalamoti*, bamboo shelves that hang from the ceiling and are ready in about five days. Both cheeses can be eaten straight away or kept for months and used for grating like *Parmesan*.

Small *denekedes*, tin containers, usually used for transporting commercial olives and *feta* cheese are also used for making *tsinogolo*. The milk and rennet are left in them for a day and night without any stirring until the concentrated *carpos* (the word means 'fruits') forms. At its centre is the soft *tsinogolo* surrounded by *tirolas*, the sour juice or whey.

is a quintessential dish of the mediterranean sun.

Cheese is another daily item. Most families keep a few goats to supply the milk for the strong, local varieties. Kyria Katina and her children are the main producers on the island. Between April and August they work hard every day; after that the animals are in kid again. Traditionally, the kids were slaughtered just before Easter – not just to signify the end of the Lenten fasting but to allow the mothers to produce milk again for the cheese-making.

Kyria Katina's children look after the goats in various meagre pastures around the island but they do not want to learn how to make the cheese for they have had enough of the long, lonely hours as goatherds. So, every morning at

If the basic diet is changing for most families, it is because they are now eating more meat and fish. The old diet was a relentless daily formula of eggs, potatoes and pulses like lentils, split peas and *fasolia* (white haricot beans). Meat used to be only eaten on Christmas day, at Easter and the one or two yearly weddings. This was supplemented by chickens, rabbits (which are no longer kept as much) and migrating wild game birds. The two favourites were *perdikes* (partridges) and *peristeria* (pigeons). In the late 1890s, rich Athenians came in their yachts to hunt them in the shooting season.

Fifteen years ago people used to wake at four in the morning to go fishing. They would go to the port and row their small boats out to sea to collect nets laid the previous evening. It was hard work rowing for a few hours but there would be fish for all the family and some would sell what they caught.

Then, eight years ago when tourism hit the island, people began to build square boxes out of cement blocks and the signs went up announcing 'Rooms for Rent'. There was suddenly no time left for traditional pursuits like fishing and people ate less fresh fish. Now, the new affluence from tourism has at least enabled them to buy engines for the boats and to find time to go fishing again on a daily basis. The butcher's shop and the advent of the fridge means that food can be kept fresh and fish caught or bought from the three commercial caiques of the island can be cleaned in the sea and taken up to the village by bus, to be eaten or frozen for another day.

While the fridge may have begun to change the eating habits of the island, the new road completed the transformation. A legendary hand-paved road, nearly 2½ miles (4km) long, once led up to the village from the port. Then it was widened and blasted with dynamite to allow a bus and trucks to follow the old and worn path of donkeys and men. Where once food spoiled on the hour-long mule ride up to the village, it can now be brought up at any time of day, giving the villagers access to a much wider range of

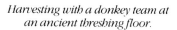

Harvesting with a donkey team at an ancient threshing floor.

food, previously only enjoyed by those in the port.

In the middle of the afternoon, a few men are winnowing wheat with donkeys on the *alonia* (threshing floors). These are paved with the grey-green slates that are still used for the floors and roofs of many houses. Families help each other with the reaping of wheat and barley, which is kept in the fields for several weeks to dry, but the threshing is done by one family alone on their own threshing floor.

A slight wind carries away all the straw and chaff, rising high into the air to cover men and donkeys in a light golden spray. Despite the heat, they need to work in the afternoon to finish this arduous task which, from a distance, seems so effortless. The wheat rises against a blue sky as the smooth, olive-wood handles of the *dihali* (three-pronged rakes) are raised like communist sickles to the sun.

By the late afternoon, some women in Chorio are sitting on the stone steps of a church, talking about the day or commenting on a tourist couple in their garish orange T-shirts. In this village of bright whitewashed houses, the only colours ever used on the woodwork are blue, green, brown and an occasional red.

Kyria Maria making dolmadakia *(stuffed vine leaves) in her courtyard.*

Old Kalliopi likes nothing better than to gossip, but her neighbour Maria is concentrating on peeling potatoes. A man like her husband, Nikos, who is due back from the fields now, expects to eat immediately. Maria will prepare something and leave it covered on the kitchen table if he is late for she also has work to do. She has to feed the chickens, water some precious parsley or celery in the kitchen garden, mend her husband's clothes or soak the mud-stained, thick woollen socks that the older men wear all the year round.

Tonight, a plate of small fried fish – *gopes* (bogues) – sent up by their daughter, married to one of the fisherman, awaits him. A bottle is on the table with two small glasses beside it, for Nikos is the largest producer of wine and someone might turn up unannounced to be proudly offered a glass of wine while he eats. His *retsina* is sold to those no longer making wine or to those who have drunk their own supplies dry.

Slowly, fathers and sons arrive back from the fields, mothers and daughters from milking the goats, and the families reunite. The donkeys have been watered and put out to graze or tethered in ruined outhouses with some hay to chew on through the long night. Outside in courtyards, icy water is pulled from the *sternes* (wells) and poured into plastic buckets and bowls. The men are washing the dirt off their tired bodies, lying exhausted on beds or already at table eating.

Water supplies are precious and cared for like a lover. The quality of life is dictated by the annual amount of rainfall that falls on the flat roofs to collect in the cisterns for everyday use and in the terraces where it softens an otherwise arid landscape with wild flowers. Even with running water now connected to the houses from the island's spring, it is still scarce enough to be rationed. Twice a week, for a few hours, the water gurgles through the pipes around the village as everyone rushes to do their washing.

The poorest woman on the island, Kyria

Left: Freshly picked wild capers ready to preserve in salt or vinegar.

Eleni, dressed in widow's black, collects *kapari* (capers) in the early evening when the flowers close and the bees and wasps are less prevalent. Picked from June until September, this trailing shrub grows all over the island, especially on the ruined walls of terraces and houses. Sprawling at the edge of a terrace beneath a church, cascading over its whitewashed walls, the white flowers with their purple stalks exude a slight perfume like that of rose. Vague though the aroma is, even at this time of day, the plants are covered in small black ants and some malevolent hornets.

Brushing away the ants, Kyria Eleni begins her laborious task. She cuts only the tops of shoots with their cluster of tiny leaves, the tightest buds and the small *kaparagoura*, cucumber-shaped fruit which are the best for pickling. The larger buds are also picked at this time of year just before they flower when they are soft and fleshy. They are boiled and eaten as a salad with chopped raw onion, olive oil and vinegar.

After an hour of handling the sometimes prickly leaves, she has a full basket and returns home. Then the sorting begins between the different buds and shoots, those that are to be soaked overnight in boiled water and those that are to be pickled.

Kyria Eleni's kitchen is like no other on the island. Cramped, narrow, some would even call it dirty. There is one window that overlooks her courtyard, filled with pots of *glistrida* (purslane) that is eaten in salads all over Greece in summer, and precious chickens hemmed in by a rickety wooden fence. Only the firewood is chopped and stacked neatly in this, the last house in Chorio without electricity or running water.

Despite the dirt and the constant hurt of her poverty, this is a kitchen inhabited by a woman immersed in the lore of the land and possessed by the ghost of her husband. Since his death she has continued to cook, as if nothing had changed, in this world of scorched garlic and blackened cooking pots.

From the ceiling hang two metal meat safes used to store food, and there is a bamboo shelf for keeping newly-made cheeses and dusty bunches of dried camomile and sage. In her old chest, she keeps her eggs and embroidery and on the cluttered table there are still two places set for the evening meal.

There are *tapsakia*, the battered metal dishes used like plates, filled with garlic cloves and small lemons, empty jars ready to make *pelte* (tomato paste) at the end of the summer and a large amphora filled with her own dark, strong olive oil. A door leads into a cave built around the rock-face. Here amphora are filled with oil, and hay and firewood are stacked on the floor. A hatch leads to the roof which is covered in sea-salt drying in the sun. But it is the fireplace with its mound of ashes and charcoal that dominates the scene. It provides heat in winter and enables Kyria Eleni always to cook quickly; lost in her world of memories, she claims to see demons leaping out of the flames. Not that she is frightened of its power, just a little mad now that she is alone. The cats are well fed in this household where too much food is cooked by force of habit.

There is always the black pot of boiling water hanging over the fire, taming the flames, just

Right: Cooking pots blackened from use over open fires.

ready for cooking. When the water has boiled, she takes it off the heat and puts the large caper buds in to soak overnight to remove the *dilitirio* (poison). Replacing the lid, she leaves them till the morning when she will boil them until soft, and eat them, once again on her own.

Picking capers is a hard task that, like all free food forages, is immensely satisfying. Something akin to a national obsession. There is always time to pick some *horta* (wild greens), *manitaria* (mushrooms), *sparangia* (asparagus) or even flowers. For those who work the land, it is one of the ways of identifying the seasons as various plants are found in secret places around the island. Discussing the year's crop of free food is also a favourite talking point in the *kafeneion* and at home.

It is evening and the two village *kafteneia*, as different in character as the two villages, are filling with men. They sit and talk, or play two popular card games, *xeri* and *pastra*, distinguished by the noisy slapping down of worn and greasy playing cards and blatant sign language between partners. A few play *tavli* (backgammon) although that game is very much identifed with the tourists in the summer months.

Those who have already eaten will drink coffee, hot chocolate or sweet liqueurs like banana or mint. The favourite soft drinks, *lemonada* or *lemonita* (both types of lemonade) and *portokalada* (like orange squash, *kokkini* is sparkling, *ble* is still), are slowly making way for more European brands like Seven Up, Fanta and Sprite. Coke and Pepsi wage their own minor skirmish, both served separately in the different *kafeneia*.

Old-fashioned *ipovrihio* 'submarines' of dipped sticky vanilla on a spoon dunked into a glass of water or *glyko koutaliou* (spooned preserves such as small bitter oranges, cherries or whole green figs), are popular with the older generation.

Then there is ouzo. Every good Greek learns how to drink vast amounts at the island parties; the trick is never to mix with any other drinks or

maybe to dance it out of the system till dawn. Whatever happens to the *kafeneion* there will always be ouzo served with a meze. But times are changing and for the younger generation it seems less a drink to stimulate the appetite and more a spirit for heavy drinking sessions.

One *kafeneion* is aged like its clientele who sit under a canopy of jasmine in the summer and listen in disbelief to the noise coming from the other. Inside, the shelves are filled with cheap, Greek-distilled gin, vodka and rum. Nobody ever touches these bottles and dust covers their look-alike labels copied from more famous brands. There are also bottles of a good Greek wine, Chateau Semeli, sadly past its prime, and somehow some Sicilian Averna, the bitter amaro beloved by catholic priests and mafia men.

A faded photograph of the singer, Donovan, stuck into the glass front of the fridge, was taken in the late sixties. It shows him when he was yachting around the Aegean, wide-eyed and long-haired, playing his guitar at an impromptu concert for some confused fishermen in the port. In those days following the semi-mystic hippy trail of Donovan and Leonard Cohen was all the rage and the islands seemed to be filled with a quieter type of tourist. All that was needed was a love bed on a deserted beach (the sleeping-bag was a far more poetic object then), a guitar and some fishing line.

Mass tourism has changed all that, of course, and the very sight of the sleeping bag or ruck-sack immediately alienates the owners from any real Greek experiences. It is presumed that they want the bars, discos and fast food that most islands now offer. This is the future drudgery that the island youth look forward to because they can see no other ways of making easy money. There is no longer work in the fields as the traditional life is abandoned.

The other *kafeneion* has been modernized with a varnished pine interior and plastic chairs but it retains its canopy of vines from which it takes its name. Klimataria, the new generation have made this their home. When his parents

A Cycladic island, with terraces that tumble down to the sea.

died, the owner Dimitris wasted no time in changing a run-down café that doubled as a barbershop into his vision of the future.

Here, the bottles are far from ersatz but the real thing. Campari, Stolichnaya, Gordons, Martini, Drambuie, Grand Marnier and Tia Maria to rival the Athens Hilton can be partnered with tonic, soda or fruit juices. Five brands of scotch and three bottled beers do the best business here, the most expensive drinks whose constant consumption is identified with a new kind of aggressive affluence.

The young generation, sons of hard-working fathers and thrifty mothers, like very loud pop music, drinking copious amounts of whisky and dreaming about *kamaki* (the summertime obsession of scoring with tourist girls). This Aegean equivalent of 'sex, drugs and rock-n-roll' keeps the place open till the early hours while the kids drink and play cards. It is not unusual for them to order whisky by the bottle, to put on their own tapes or tune the radio into the local pop station from Syros, Aegeo FM, and turn the evening into an impromptu disco before staggering home through the quiet streets.

The pride of the *kafeneon* is its hand-painted menu outside the door. On one side the menu is in Greek and on the other, an extraordinary English translation which has been copied word-for-word by all the other places in the port. It offers hamburgers, spaghetti, pork chops, shrimps, meatballs, ink-stands (its translation for *kalamarakia* [squid]), olish variety (for *pikilia*, a mixture of hot and cold *mezedes*) and milk pie (for *galaktoboureko*, a Greek custard slice), but it usually only serves pizzas.

To this new generation, these pizzas are another local symbol of sophistication and wealth. They are an everyday sight in the cities but somehow take on a new meaning in this small community. Those that eat, or are offered a slice, become unwitting pawns in the battle for change. Those that refuse are conservative examples of the old islander. Although these are actually very good pizzas, they are just another reason why tourists

Church bells that call the faithful to daily services.

feel so cheated when they search for real Greek food.

The new generation are true rebels without a cause. Frequently sent to Athens or Syros to learn a trade like plumbing, they return to find there is no such work at home. They end up doing day-rate jobs, like whitewashing or building, to earn money for their evenings out. Living at home, they never learn to cook or fend for themselves. If they are lucky, they marry an island bride with a house and *prika* (dowry) and the circle remains unbroken.

They can stay on the island, which many want to do after a brief sample of the rat-race in the polluted capital Athens, if they can find work for the future, which may prove difficult. There are already too many electricians, plumbers and fishermen trying to make a living. Perhaps the only solution is tourism in a more durable, refined form. But any gentrification ultimately creates a hollow place like Mykonos or Santorini where most links with the past have been forgotten or bastardized into evenings of folk dancing, plate smashing and a neon wasteland of kebab-houses.

Not everyone visits the *kafeneons*. The new affluence has enabled people to buy televisions, still a novelty on the island. The *vegera*, after-dinner visits, between families where the women knit and the men drink some wine and talk before bed, may often be spent in front of the TV.

If it is harvest time, most people go to bed early. In winter months, too, the rain and wind howling through the narrow streets keep the families at home, for who really wants to get soaked walking from one village to the other just for an hour's conversation?

On this island, where hard work in the fields is punctuated by rare celebrations like a wedding or baptism, the *glenti* (village dance) is a time to drink and dance till dawn. It used to continue for two days and nights, with all the village bringing food and drink. The musicians would play violin and lute or *tsabouna* (primitive bagpipes) made from a goat's skin and

drum, but now loudspeakers crackle with a medley of island tunes.

Holidays are unheard of; childhood is considered a semi-vacation but for the rest of one's life the good things are found on a daily basis. Some men and women have never left the island. Their world relies on good weather for their crops, not on the politics of change. They need little but a plate and glass for some simple island food and wine.

This July day ends as it began with a silence broken only by a ghetto blaster, the proud possession of a young man who has just returned from military service. The moon that shines on the prickly pears by the chapel in the cemetery, between the two villages of Chorio and Castro, also illuminates the gravestones of an earlier generation. It is this generation that benefited most from living off the land. Their poverty meant trading their produce; honey for cheese, olive oil for goat's meat, wheat for wool. But, in most cases, they were self-sufficient and their diet reflected the purity of such a life. On many tombstones, the ages are over eighty and on half a dozen they are over a hundred. Testimony to the wisdom of simple peasant food on this small and barren Cycladic island.

Dolmadakia

Stuffed vine leaves

At Easter, during the Lenten fasting, these are made as in this recipe. At other times, meat is used in the filling, with *avgolemono* sauce.

SERVES 6
50 vine (grape) leaves, preferably fresh
2 medium-sized onions, finely chopped
30 ml/2 tbsp olive oil
45 ml/3 tbsp finely chopped fresh dill
15 ml/1 tbsp finely chopped fresh mint
225 g/8 oz/1⅓ cups long-grain rice
2 large tomatoes, skinned and chopped
salt and freshly ground black pepper
600 ml/1 pint/2½ cups water

If using fresh vine (grape) leaves, blanch them in boiling water for 5 minutes and drain; if using preserved leaves, soak in hot water and rinse several times. Sauté the onions in the olive oil, adding the dill, mint and then the rice. After 5 minutes, add the tomatoes and simmer for another 5 minutes. Season to taste.

Take 15 ml/1 tbsp of the mixture and place in the centre of a vine (grape) leave. Fold the ends over until completely wrapped. As each *dolmadakia* is made, place it in a circle at the bottom of a large saucepan. Make sure they are tightly packed in the pot.

Add the water to cover and put a plate with a weight on top so that they do not split. Simmer for 1 hour. Serve hot or cold.

Militinia

Easter pastries Cycladic island style

SERVES 6-8 OR ABOUT 24 PASTRIES
450 g/1 lb *mezithra* or soft cheese like *ricotta*
450 g/1 lb/2¼ cups caster (US granulated) sugar
3-4 drops vanilla essence (extract)
2 eggs beaten
450 g/1 lb/3¼ cups plain (all-purpose) flour
90 ml/6 tbsp/3 oz olive oil
30-45 ml/2-3 tbsp water

Preheat the oven to 180°C/350°F/Gas Mark 4.

Put the cheese into a bowl and beat the lumps out. Add the sugar, eggs and vanilla essence, mix well and then bind with a pinch of flour.

In another bowl, make the pastry: sift the flour through a fine sieve and then add the olive oil into the centre of the flour and begin to make the dough. Knead, gradually adding as much water as required. Sprinkle some extra flour onto a large flat surface and roll the pastry as thinly as possible with a rolling pin.

Cut circles with a wine glass that is 30 cm/3½ inch in diameter. Then pinch the sides upwards to make octagonal-shaped cases. Put the pastries onto an oiled baking tray and then add a tablespoon of the filling to each, making sure that they are not overfilled.

Bake for 30 to 40 minutes until golden brown. Allow to cool and serve. The pastries will keep for a few days.

Militinia, *Easter cakes made with soft cheese, are a Cycladic island speciality.*

Easter Salad Island Style

Green salad

SERVES 4

1 lollo rosso or cos (romaine) lettuce, washed
and very finely sliced
4-5 spring onions (scallions), including stems,
finely sliced
45 ml/3 tbsp chopped fresh dill
45 ml/3 tbsp olive oil
15 ml/1 tbsp red wine vinegar
salt and freshly ground black pepper

Put the finely sliced lettuce in a salad bowl,
add the spring onions (scallions) and then the
dill. Add oil, vinegar and seasoning. Serve
immediately.

Summer Salad Island Style

Tomato, potato, onion and caper salad

SERVES 2-4

2 large ripe tomatoes, sliced
2 large potatoes, peeled, boiled and sliced
1 medium-sized onion, sliced
30 ml/2 tbsp pickled capers
30 ml/2 tbsp olive oil
15 ml/1 tbsp red wine vinegar
salt and freshly ground black pepper

Lay the tomatoes, potatoes and onion in a flat
dish. Sprinkle the capers on top and then add
the oil, vinegar and seasoning.

Kolokythia Gemista Me Avgolemono

Stuffed courgettes with *avgolemono* sauce

SERVES 4

900 g/2 lb large, pale green courgettes
(zucchini), available at Greek food shops.
450 g/1 lb minced (ground) beef
2 medium-sized onions, chopped or grated
75 g/2½ oz/½ cup long/grain rice
30 ml/2 tbsp finely chopped fresh flat leafed
parsley
15 ml/1 tbsp chopped fresh mint
about 600 ml/1 pint/2½ cups stock or water
45 ml/3 tbsp olive oil or butter
salt and freshly ground black pepper
2 eggs, beaten
juice of 1 lemon

Wash and scoop out the courgette (zucchini)
flesh, taking care not to break the sides (it is best
to use an apple corer or a long handled
teaspoon). Sprinkle with salt. Mix the meat,
onions, rice and herbs together and use to stuff
the courgettes (zucchini). Do not overstuff as the
vegetables might split.

Place in a large saucepan and pour over
enough stock to cover. Add the olive oil or
butter and seasoning. Place a weighted plate on
top and simmer for 1 hour.

Remove from the heat. With the stock,
eggs and lemon juice, make *avgolemono* sauce
(see page 80) and shake into the pan. Serve
immediately.

Moustalevria
Grape must dessert

This is always made during the grape harvest, from the grape must traditionally cleared with *stakti* (wood ash). The quick version uses cornflour (cornstarch) instead of flour and commercial grape juice which needs no clearing. The result after refrigeration should be a jelly-like consistency.

SERVES 4

60 ml/4 tbsp cornflour (cornstarch)
15 ml/1 tbsp sugar
750 ml/1¼ pints/3 cups grape juice
45 ml/3 tbsp sesame seeds
ground cinnamon

Mix the cornflour (cornstarch) and sugar together in a bowl. Bring the grape juice to the boil. Slowly mix one-quarter of the juice with the cornflour (cornstarch) mixture, then stir this into the remaining juice in the saucepan. Cook, stirring, until it thickens. Take off the heat immediately and pour into individual bowls. Sprinkle sesame seeds and cinnamon on top and leave to cool, then refrigerate to set.

Sfovgato
Eggs and tomatoes

SERVES 4

4 large ripe tomatoes
5 ml/1 tsp sugar (if tomatoes are not ripe)
45 ml/3 tbsp olive oil
6 eggs
salt and freshly ground black pepper

Wash and coarsely chop the tomatoes. Add to a large frying pan, with the sugar if used, and cook over a medium heat in their own liquid for 30 minutes. When they are soft and most of the liquid has evaporated, add the olive oil and cook for 5 minutes longer. Then add the eggs, and salt and pepper to taste and stir continuously until the eggs are almost set. Some people prefer to beat the eggs lightly before mixing, but most islanders insist that the secret of this dish is to stir them directly in and mix while cooking.

Skordalia
Garlic dip

This is always served with fried *bakaliaros* (salt cod) and *melitzanes*, *kolokythia* and *patsaria*. It is commonly made with potato, bread or nuts like almonds and walnuts. This version uses walnuts, and the vinegar gives it a pinkish colour.

SERVES 4-6

5-6 garlic cloves, peeled
75 g/2½ oz/¾ cup skinned walnuts
2 thick slices of stale bread, crusts removed
75-90 ml/5-6 tbsp olive oil
30 ml/2 tbsp red wine vinegar
salt and freshly ground black pepper

Pound the garlic in a mortar, then add the walnuts and pound together. Soak the bread in water for 15 minutes; squeeze excess moisture out and add to the garlic and walnuts. Continue blending until a smooth paste is formed, slowly adding the oil and vinegar at the same time. Add salt and pepper at the end, to taste.

Fishing in The Aegean

Above: *A boat painted with the figure of Poseidon.*
Left: *Laying nets.*

Although the Aegean is overworked by the commercial fishermen, it is still possible to catch many fish with spearguns or lines which the humble nets of the caique never touch.

Summer sees the Italians, always obsessive about their diving, descend upon the Aegean with expensive inflatables, illegal oxygen tanks, state-of-the-art airguns and designer wetsuits. Their greed is never popular with the Greeks who are equally obsessed with the sport. The government now imposes a daily quota on fish like *rophos* (grouper) in order to protect the diminishing stocks of fish but it is near-impossible to impose.

The Aegean, lying as it does at the end of the Mediterranean, feels the influence of both the Black Sea and the Red Sea via the Suez Canal. This is reflected in the migrating seasonal fish like *tonnos* (tuna), *xiphios* (swordfish), *gofari* (blue fish), *palamida* (bonito), *mayatico* (amberjack), *kynigos* (dolphin fish) and *frissa* (shad).

Through the Suez Canal such fish as the unappetizing *germanos* (rabbit fish) have established themselves in the Dodecanese islands. Large shoals of this jet-black, spiky fish can be seen, whose colour drains to a deathly cold silver when caught.

The Dodecanese and north Aegean islands like Chios, Mitilini and Samothrace, near to the Turkish coast, benefit from being close to the migratory paths of fish. Mitilini is well known for its sardines from the Gulf of Kaloni, canned and salted after being trapped during the spring months and in remote Kastellorizo (otherwise known as Megisti), dolphin fish is abundant in late September. The islanders rush to be outside the harbour in order to spin for this, the most beautiful fish in the Aegean, with its rainbow colours of blue, yellow and green that fade as soon as it is taken from the line.

Every taverna in the harbour grills these delicious fish with flesh that tastes like a cross between tuna and veal. Some people dry them in the sun to warm later over charcoal as *mezedes*, others salt them for winter use.

Salpes (a type of bream) ready to be sold in the market.

In contrast, the Cyclades suffer from their proximity to Athens and the heavy influx of tourists and seem to have much less fish. Many fish are sent to the Piraeus market, much caught to satisfy local demand. The summer months are also the worst time for fishing. The large shoals only return in the spring and autumn when all the tourists have migrated home.

On the north side of this island, there is a steep path that leads down to the cliffs below the village. Here, the sea stretches out to other islands, Paros and Antiparos, Naxos and Sifnos. The water is deep and the villagers wary of this part of the coast joke that there are monsters and sharks. Ten years ago there used to be *fokies*, Aegean seal, around these cliffs but all such 'monsters' have now disappeared. They are now protected in a reserve off Alonissos, in the Northern Sporades. But, like many things in Greece, this measure is too late a gesture to save the hundreds lost in the fishermen's nets.

There is one small cove which the old caique that used to bring the mail and seasick passengers from Ios was sometimes forced to make for when it was impossible to anchor in the port. A small rowing boat would come out and donkeys would be waiting to take everyone up the hill.

The islanders still come down to these rocks to collect *alati physiko* the crystals of strong sea salt or to catch *kalamarakia* (squid). In the winter, in the early evening, lines with spiky lures are put off the rocks and when the squid are brought close enough a wooden stick with curled nails slits the large ones out of the sea. Some can be up to 1.5 kilos (3 lb) in weight and it is not uncommon to catch 10-12 kilos (22-26 lb) in a few hours.

The best fishing is underwater where the cliff face honeycombs into deep crevasses and narrow rivulets of rock. Before it darkens into the depths at less than 20 m (61 ft), the sea is perfect for diving.

Red and grey *skari* (parrot fish, their name comes aptly from the Ancient Greek 'scairo' to leap) somersault and chase through the rocks.

Right: Classic mezedes; baby octopus, boiled and served with oil and vinegar, and karavides *(Dublin Bay prawns) that are usually grilled.*

The Greeks like to bake or grill them whole without scaling or cleaning them for the insides are considered a delicacy. *Skaros* is at its best in summer and one old recipe, according to Archestratus in *Gastronomy*, was to bake it with cheese and oil, salt and sesame seeds.

There are some fish like the highly prized *synagrida* (dentex), blue-grey *mayatico* (amberjack), *loutsos* (barracuda) and *zargana* (garfish) with its thin backbone that turns emerald green when cooked, that are just too fast and wily to be caught with a spear gun. They are caught with spinning lines and if a fisherman is lucky he will sometimes bring in a large dentex that has strayed in from the deep and proudly show it off in the port.

Two fish that swim in fast, confusing shoals are *kephalos* (grey mullet) and *salpes*. This last has distinctive yellow stripes along its body and can be trapped in holes. It is a prolific seaweed eater and often has a bloated, stinking stomach which needs careful cleaning, stripping the black inside skin clean away. Stuffed with wild thyme and sea-salt, *salpa* are best baked in the oven.

Perka (sea perch), *chiloutsa* (wrasse), *pontikos* (forkbeard), that tastes like hake, small red *scorpena* (scorpion fish) and the darker *skorpios* all lurk underneath the shallower rocks and are best in fish soups like *psarosoupa* or *kakavia*. Two other fish esteemed in Ancient Greece, the *selaki* (ray), and *barbounia* (red mullet), are also found here.

The Greeks refer to all rays by the common name of *selaki* although there are actually three types caught in the Aegan. *Selaki* or *megalo selaki* (large ray) is the thornback ray; and *aetos* is the huge eagle ray with its long and tail and flapping horns near its eyes. This is sometimes caught in the deep water between Ikaria and Patmos in the Dodecanese. *Moudiastra* is the electric ray and is often found around the island gliding in from the deep, an eerie sight as it rests on the bottom camouflaged as a flat rock. The Ancient Greek word for it was *narki* after the numbling effect administered by the electric

shock in its tail. These rays are all fried although Archestratus suggests that it should be 'stewed in oil, wine, fragrant herbs with a little grated cheese'.

There are two species of red mullet, *barbounia* and *koutsomoura*, the one more expensive than the other. *Barbounia* is redder with a rounder face, longer barbs and faint stripes on its body; *koutsomoura* is a paler yellow-pink colour with shorter barbs and its name refers to its chiselled profile. It is easy to be cheated in tavernas if this difference is not known when choosing the fish, harder still after they have been fried. *Barbounia* has the sweeter flesh of the two.

Greeks and tourists are mad about this fish, hence their expense, only justified if they are really fresh. The Romans and Ancient Greeks also adored the fish. Roman gourmets were so obsessed with the larger sort, they kept them in captivity. But the Greeks liked the fish (called *triglie* because it spawned three times a year) more for its religious significance. As Plato explains, it was sacred to the goddess Hecate: 'For she is the goddess of the three ways and looks three ways, and they offer her meals on the thirtieth day.' Another classical writer declares it's contraceptive powers if a woman or man drank the wine in which a mullet had been drowned.

Further along the coast, where the cliffs crumble into the sea at *Mavri Spilia* (Black Caves), a series of underwater caves and boulders with spring water trickling out of them make the perfect hiding place for *karavida* or *lyra* the flat lobster. The favourite way to eat these is grilled over charcoal as *meze* for they have a sweeter flavour than *astakos* (lobster) and go well with ouzo. There are not as many octopus as in the northern Aegean, especially the Sporades, but a large, brooding octopus will sometimes swim out of its lair. They are cooked

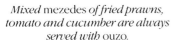

Mixed mezedes *of fried prawns, tomato and cucumber are always served with* ouzo.

A fisherman from Skiathos with his newly-caught octopus.

such as spurge and mullein to poison the water and stun the fish, netting them when they floated to the surface. Large *rophos* or the pinker *sphirida*, another member of the grouper family, can be baked in the oven but the Greeks prefer to use the smaller fish in soups.

When the fish is cleaned back at the cove, a *smerna* (moray eel) may emerge from its nearby hole to nibble at the guts and scales. Its ferocious teeth and glazed eyes rear out of its purple head giving it an ugly, crazed look. The moray often makes its home near an octopus hole and when desperate for food will snack on its tentacles.

There is nothing better than these fresh fish caught all over the Aegean. If they are the lifeblood of that sea and offer a livelihood for many islanders, they are also one of the most direct links with the past, echoing that ancient civilization in both fishing techniques and love of fresh fish in the daily diet.

The ways in which they are eaten remain the same: baked or grilled, salted or dried. The Ancient Greeks used to wrap a belly of tuna in fig leaves and bury it in hot embers. Now foil is used but the technique is unchanged. The favourite way of eating fish in *mezedes* derives from the ancient *opson* (the small plates of different relishes).

Kakavia was the soup that most people believe to be the humble forerunner to *bouillabaise*, introduced into France by the maritime Greeks. It was made then with herbs, salt, water, olive oil and caraway seeds. Today it may contain tomatoes or potatoes (which had not then been brought over from the New World) but it is still traditionally made on fishing caiques as they make their way back to port in the evening.

In the central *Athinas* market in Athens, the stalls that do the best business are those that sell the caiques' catch. Their signs announce proudly 'We sell Aegean fish' or 'These are one hundred per cent Greek fish', for much is brought in from Israel, Brazil and the Far East to cater for the thousands in the holiday hotels and have the tell-tale grey bones of frozen fish when cooked.

in stews with onions (*octapodi me kremithia* or with rice or pasta (*oktapodi pilafi*). Smaller octopuses are always grilled on charcoal.

There is one fish that every diver dreams of catching: the big *rophos*. In the late afternoon they come out of their holes in the rocks to sun and search lazily for food but if seen will run back into hiding. Some stay in the same holes for years, growing larger each season and unable to be teased out. When they do emerge there may only be time for one good shot and then the battle begins. An easy method, favoured by impatient Greeks, is to squirt ammonia into the hole to force the fish out. Old fishermen used *flomos*; mountain herbs with toxic properties

Arni Sto Fourno Me Patates or Hilopittes

Roast Easter Lamb 'island style'

Lamb is traditionally baked in a *tapsi*, with potatoes or *hilopittes* (egg noodles) placed around the meat to cook in the juices. *Hilopittes* are available from Greek food shops. If using them, they must be put in with the meat 45 minutes before the end of cooking, with enough water to just cover the pasta (it will absorb all the liquid). At Easter, it is more customary to serve potatoes.

SERVES 6

**1.8-2.2 kg/4-5 lb leg of lamb
2 garlic cloves, sliced
juice of 2 lemons
salt and freshly ground black pepper
75-90 ml/5-6 tbsp olive oil
30 ml/2 tbsp dried oregano, or chopped fresh herbs (thyme, rosemary or mint) if preferred
1.4 kg/3 lb potatoes, peeled and quartered, or 500 g/1 lb packet of hilopittes
about 600 ml/1 pint/2½ cups water**

Preheat the oven to 200°C/400°F/Gas Mark 6. Score the lamb and press garlic into the cuts; alternatively add the garlic to the potatoes. Rub the meat with the juice of ½ lemon and salt and place in a roasting tin with the olive oil. Sprinkle with pepper and oregano or fresh herbs. If potatoes are used instead of pasta, place them around the meat with half of the water and the rest of the lemon juice.

Turn the heat down to mark 180°C/350°F/Gas Mark 4 and roast for 1½-2 hours. Check from time to time and add more water to the potatoes if necessary. Serve with Easter 'island stuffing' and salad.

Arni Fricassée

Lamb fricassée

SERVES 4-6

**900 g/2 lb shoulder or leg of lamb (ask the butcher to chop through to the bone 4-6 times)
10 spring onions (scallions), finely chopped
45 ml/3 tbsp olive oil
salt and freshly ground black pepper
2 large frisée (curly endive), quartered, or 2 cos (romaine) lettuce, coarsely shredded
45 ml/3 tbsp coarsely chopped fresh dill
2 eggs, beaten
juice of 1 lemon**

Wash the meat. In a large flameproof casserole dish, sauté the spring onions (scallions) in the oil and then add the meat to brown. Add enough water to cover the meat and seasoning to taste and simmer, covered, for 1 hour.

Add the frisée (endive) or lettuce and dill to the casserole and cook for a further 30 minutes or until the meat is tender and the sauce reduced. (Some cooks add the lettuce or endive, earlier).

Remove from the heat. Make an *avgolemono* sauce with some of the stock, the eggs and lemon juice (see page 80) and shake back into the casserole. Serve immediately.

Melitzanosalata

Aubergine dip

SERVES 4

**450 g/1 lb (2 medium-sized) aubergines (eggplants)
2-3 garlic cloves, peeled
30 ml/2 tbsp skinned walnuts
60 ml/4 tbsp olive oil
15 ml/1 tbsp vinegar**

salt and freshly ground black pepper
1 onion, coarsely chopped (optional)
1 medium-sized tomato, skinned and coarsely chopped (optional)

Preheat the oven to 180°C/350°F/Gas Mark 4. Bake the aubergines (eggplants) in the oven for 1 hour or until soft. When cool, peel off the skins and scoop out the flesh. Place in a colander, sprinkle with salt and press excess liquid out, or leave to drain covered with a small plate weighted down.

Pound the garlic and nuts to a paste with a pestle. In a mixing bowl, add the pounded garlic to the aubergines (egg plants). Pound until smooth, then slowly work in the oil, vinegar and seasoning. Add the onion and tomato if using. Refrigerate the mixture for a few hours before eating.

Octapodi Me Kremithia

Octopus with onions

Octopus is cooked in a variety of stew styles – with wine, tomatoes, macaroni or rice.

SERVES 4
900 g/2 lb small octopus
45 ml/3 tbsp olive oil
3 large onions, sliced
2 large tomatoes, skinned and chopped
15 ml/1 tbsp tomato paste, dissolved in
175 ml/6 fl oz/¾ cup warm water
15 ml/1 tbsp chopped fresh flat-leafed parsley
salt and freshly ground black pepper
450 ml/¾ pint/2 cups water

Wash the octopus and clean if necessary. Heat a large saucepan on a low flame and place the octopus in it to evaporate some of its juices for 5 minutes. Remove the octopus and cut into cubes.

Heat the oil in the saucepan and sauté the onions for 5 minutes. Then add the octopus, tomatoes and other ingredients. Cover with the water and simmer for 1-1½ hours until tender, checking occasionally if it needs more water. The sauce should be thick at the end.

Bakaliaros Yiachni

Stewed salt-cod

Bakaliaros is fried and served with *skordalia*, made into *keftedes* or stewed 'yiachni' style with the addition of *horta* by some cooks. This is the traditional recipe made more 'Turkish' by the addition of raisins and pine-nuts.

SERVES 4-6
900 g/2 lb salt cod
2 large onions, sliced
60-75 ml/4-5 tbsp olive oil
2 garlic cloves, finely sliced
60 ml/4 tbsp tomato paste
½ glass of white wine
30 ml/2 tbs raisins (optional)
30 ml/2 tbsp pine nuts (optional)
freshly ground black pepper
1.2 litres/2 pints/5 cups water

Soak the salt cod overnight, or for a minimum of 12 hours, in as many changes of water as possible. Rinse, cut into large pieces and remove the skin and bones.

In a large saucepan, sauté the onions in the olive oil, add the garlic, tomato, paste and wine and fry together for 5 minutes. Add the salt cod, with the raisins and pine nuts if using and black pepper to taste. Cover with the water and simmer on a low heat for 30 minutes until the sauce thickens. Alternatively, bake in a preheated 180°C/350°F/Gas Mark 4 oven.

Sardelles Sto Fourno

Baked sardines

Fresh anchovies are also used for this dish.

SERVES 4-6

900 g/2 lb fresh sardines
5-6 garlic cloves, finely sliced
45 ml/3 tbsp finely chopped fresh flat-leafed parsley
45 ml/3 tbsp olive oil
175 ml/6 fl oz/¾ cup water
juice of 1 lemon
15 ml/1 tbsp dried oregano
salt and freshly ground black pepper

Preheat the oven to 180°C/350°F/Gas Mark 4.

Clean, gut and rinse the sardines. Put in a shallow baking dish and add the garlic and parsley, evenly spread. Mix the oil, water, lemon juice, oregano and seasoning and pour over the sardines. Bake in the oven for 20-30 minutes.

Kakavia

Fish soup

SERVES 4

900 g/2 lb small fish (preferably rock fish like *rascasse*, wrasse)
2 medium-sized onions, sliced
3 large potatoes, peeled and quartered
45 ml/3 tbsp chopped available fresh herbs like parsley and celery tops
60 ml/4 tbsp olive oil
1 large tomato, skinned and chopped (optional)
2 carrots, peeled and sliced (optional)
salt and freshly ground black pepper
1.2 litres/2 pints/5 cups water
juice of 1 lemon

Clean and gut the fish and place in a large saucepan with all the other ingredients except the lemon juice. Simmer for 40 minutes.

Remove the fish into bowls. Add the lemon juice to the soup, stir and either pour over the fish or serve separately.

Soupies Me Spanaki

Cuttlefish with spinach

SERVES 4

700 g/1½ lb cuttlefish or squid
60 ml/4 tbsp olive oil
1 large onion, sliced
175 ml/6 fl oz/¾ cup white wine
15 ml/1 tbsp tomato paste, dissolved in 175 ml/ 6 fl oz/¾ cup water, or 4 small tomatoes, skinned and chopped
30 ml/2 tbsp chopped fresh flat-leafed parsley
salt and freshly ground black pepper
1.4 kg/3 lb fresh spinach, washed and coarsely chopped

Clean the cuttlefish (or squid if using), removing beak, eyes and backbone. Wash again, then cut into strips. Heat the olive oil in a saucepan and sauté the onion until it browns. Add the fish and cook until it begins to brown. Then add the wine, tomato paste mixture or tomatoes, 15 ml/ 1 tbsp parsley, seasoning to taste and some water to cover everything. Leave to simmer for 1 hour.

When soft, add the spinach and cook for another 10 minutes. Sprinkle over the remaining parsley before serving.

Fassoulada

Bean soup

SERVES 4

**450 g/1 lb/2⅔ cups dried haricot beans (Great
Northern or other white beans)
1.75 litres/3 pints/7½ cups water
1 large onion, coarsely chopped
2 carrots, peeled and sliced
1 stalk celery and celery tops, sliced and diced
2 ripe tomatoes, skinned and roughly chopped
30 ml/2 tbsp tomato paste
75-90 ml/5-6 tbsp olive oil**

**1 bay leaf
salt and freshly ground black pepper
30 ml/2 tbsp chopped fresh flat-leafed parsley**

Soak the beans overnight in cold water. Drain and rinse, then cover with the fresh measured water in a large saucepan. Bring to the boil and skim any foam from the surface with a spoon. Add all the other ingredients and simmer for 2-3 hours or until tender. Add more water if needed during cooking to make sure all the ingredients are just covered.

Pour into soup bowls, garnish with chopped parsley on top and serve.

Preparing fassoulada *(bean soup) a staple one-pot classic of the Greek diet.*

Other Islands in the Sun

Above: *Small fishing boats in Tilos.* Left: *Thera, the dramatic cliff-top capital of Santorini.*

**Three rocks, a few burnt pines,
an abandoned chapel and
farther above
the same landscape repeated
starts again;**

**George Seferis from
*Mythical Story***

If the food of the islands remains unchanged, so does the way of reaching them. There are probably as many ferries as there are islands in Greece and many that have gone are mourned as lost friends such as the *Kyknos* (Swan), the legendary workhorse of the Sporades with its rusting white paint and narrow deck, that plied the route from Aghios Konstantinos to Trikeri, Skiathos, Skopolos, Alonissos, Skyros and Kimi on the eastern coast of Evia. Now there are landing craft crossing continually to Evia and Aegina or the more sophisticated orange and blue Flying Dolphins that flit across to the Saronic and Sporadic islands in half the time it used to take.

There are also the new generation of ships like the Milos or the Georgos Express, ex-cross channel ferries that go out in any weather loaded down with lorries and cars; or the small Scandinavian fjord boats that labour in a sudden storm with fine wooden panelling, covering the lesser Cycladic islands like Heraklia, Schinoussa and Donoussa. There are cruise ships that flatter Mykonos, Rhodes, Patmos and Santorini with weekly visits and finally, scattered across a sea that has seen a thousand shipwrecks and sails splitting in the ever-changing winds, there is that scarred and battered emblem of the Aegean, the caique.

Caiques are everywhere, making fast and furious for safe harbours and secluded bays before nightfall. Overweight fishing caiques, all barnacled and peeling paint, hurrying the best of their catches back for the overnight ferries to Piraeus. Crushing huge blocks of ice, packing the lobster and red mullet into wooden cases, the fishermen pass them to familiar faces in the hold, tearing the covers of cigarette packs to address the cases to their regular fishmongers in the markets of Athens.

Fast caiques with loudspeakers vibrating in the rigging bring the tourists back after a day at the beach, their greedy owners standing at the gangplanks taking the 100 drachmae bills. Smuggling caiques in the Dodecanese meet up with Turkish kayiks in the middle of the night to transfer their cargoes of cigarettes in return for coffee and even bread. There are *fortiga*, caiques that take vital supplies of water, diesel and paraffin to the barren islands like Fourni, Psara, Kastellorizo and Agios Efstratios, their captains exchanging cheap radios for kilos of honey and olive oil. And there is the daily caique from Koufonissia to Naxos carrying the mail and passengers to connect with the regular ferry.

The caique is still the most enduring symbol of life and death in the Aegean and the poetics of the sea in Greek life are constantly celebrated in literature and poetry, music and art, especially in the folk songs of the Dodecanese islands and the much imitated paintings of the naïve artist, Katsas of Aegina.

It is also living proof of the proud and insular nature of all Greek islands and their ability to survive whatever the weather. When the scheduled ferries are forced to stay in port, the workhorse caique continues its perilous journey, built to survive the worst storms of the Aegean. One thing remains constant: the need to sail and fish the Aegean as if to reaffirm through the symbolism of the catch itself the daily battle with the elements and the survival of the real, unconquered soul of Greece in the life of its islanders. A familiar sight at every quayside are the weather-beaten faces of the fishermen as they haggle over their catch with persistent women or mend nets in the afternoon sun.

In a one-caique island like Arki, opposite Patmos, the nets of the fishing family camouflage their house by the shore. They receive their

Right: Off-loading locals and their bulky luggage at islands without a quay is often precarious in the winter time.

Fishing boat moored in the shallow cove of Arki opposite Patmos.

bread, supplies and visitors from Patmos in the summertime and cheerfully turn their humble home into a taverna. The narrow cove that leads to their house (and a few summer huts built by relations who come in the warm weather) bring shoals of *kefalous* (grey mullet) into the shallow waters and their round metal traps baited with stale bread. The owner, Dimitris, rows out into the shallows and brings the fish back, cleans them and gives them to his wife to grill or fry. If he is out fishing, his wife will run round to her cherished chickens and find eggs to fry, the stand-by dish all over Greece when unexpected visitors arrive.

Around the Dodecanese and Cycladic islands, there are many semi-deserted islands like Levitha, Sirna, Tria Nisia, Antikeros and Farmakonisi used as stopping points in rough weather or as a base for week-long fishing expeditions by travelling caiques from Kalymnos or Koufonissia, both islands renowned for the wanderlust of their sea captains. There are sometimes solitary shepherds who also make their summer homes here, tending their flocks and fishing from their small boats, who will always share their scarce food and drink, glad for some company for a few hours. In Farmakonisi, north-east of Kalymnos and close to the Turkish coast, an old abandoned farmhouse is in ruins after a World War Two fighter plane, that lies rusting nearby, crashed into it. Yet people still visit the island from time to time to make sure, because of its proximity to Turkey, that it remains in Greek possession by leaving goats there and some simple signs of habitation: a restored well and bucket, a white-washed chapel and tattered Greek flag flying in the wind.

In Antikeros, an old shepherd and fisherman goes every week from his home on Koufonissia, one of the flattest of the lesser Cycladic islands, to check on his goats. He takes his supplies with him: potatoes, onions, carrots, rice, lemons, water, wine and bread. All he need do is catch some fish and he has the ingredients for *kakavia*, the classic fish soup of the Aegean. In his small hut, he keeps firewood and a large blackened saucepan into which he pours some precious water although it is not uncommon to use a little sea-water when supplies are low. If he is lucky enough to have caught a medium-sized *skorpio* (scorpion fish) he cuts it into three and throws it into the pot with potatoes or rice, onions, olive oil, salt and pepper. Otherwise he uses small sea perch, or the beautiful pink and blue striped *katsoula* (a type of wrasse) with its chiselled face. Once the fire is alight and the water is boiling, it takes about 40 minutes to cook. If he is really hungry, he breaks lumps of bread into the soup to thicken it before pouring it into an old earthenware bowl and squeezing the juice of half a lemon on top. He sits outside his hut on stone, the tame goats coming closer and the gulls diving into the calm sea below, eating silently with the smell of wild thyme all around him. In the distance lies Keros, once capital during the ancient Cycladic period (with

Waiting for visitors and supplies in Arki are the old couple who always open their house as a make-shift taverna when required.

its impressive archaeological finds now in Athens museums), also overrun by goats. Beyond Keros is the shepherd's home Koufonissia, an island of fishermen (whose ancestors are reputed to have all been pirates), caiques and tractors, the local means of land transport. Even the priest has his own small caique and discusses where the shoals of fish are over his two-wave radio. When the old man returns, he is also on the radio to any caique that is listening, asking them to tell his wife he is coming home. 'Tell her I want to eat meat and salad tonight', he calls down the crackling line.

At Anidro, half-way between Astipalea and Ios as the crow flies, a desolate rock with some of the best spear-fishing in the Aegean for few people ever go there, there are two caiques from Kalymnos. They are moored together like illicit lovers sheltering from the storm. Both are similar to gypsy caravans, every available space is taken up with fishing nets and tackle, baskets and the tell-tale signs that these are the long-distance caiques of sponge fishermen, the wet-suits and black plastic bag flags pinned to long poles. These are used as floats, tied to the baited hooks and lines when deep-water fishing for *xiphia* (swordfish), the other occupation undertaken on long voyages when conditions are right. There are large, cleaned sponges drying in the rigging and others, still black and waiting to be cleaned out of the milky juices that have to be squeezed out, are dangled on ropes in the water.

Cleaning nets of tiny atherina *(smelt) in Koufonissia.*

Above: *A Kalymniot caique with sponges drying in the rigging.*
Above right: *Empty plastic oil bottles are used as buoys and markers for deep-water fishing for swordfish.*

If the sea is calm, these are towed behind from port to port to clean them and so that their strong smell on the cramped caiques does not lead to mutiny. In the past, the sponge-fishermen travelled as far as Cyprus and Libya in search of good hunting grounds; an incredibly feat in such small craft. For six months, Pothea, the main harbour in Kalymnos, is empty except for tourists. Then at the end of the fishing season, the caiques slowly return and the *kafeneia* are alive again with fishing tales from the Deep and the strong smell of cigarettes fills the air. The quayside is lined with fish tavernas and their small displays outside lit by solitary electric light bulbs. Inside every one there is a sea captain celebrating his return with his family and friends.

Tonight in Anidro, one of the crew plays the *bouzouki* while they drink ouzo to keep warm. They share their bounty from the day's diving for *mezedes*, delicacies like *fouskies* (violets), *anemones* (sea anemones), *achinous* (sea urchins) and *pinnes* (razor clams), all with the unmistakable strong iodine taste of the sea. *Pinnes* (razor clams) are also pickled with oil and vinegar and kept on board. In the small galley, with no more than a primus stove, a large saucepan and frying pan, someone is preparing fried *barbounia* (red mullet) for the two crews. 'Bring them quickly before the wind blows us to Africa', the captain calls from the deck.

At every port in Greece, there are men selling food and drink to last minute passengers. Nutsellers with their carts overloaded with *fistikia* (pistachio) from Aegina, *passatempo* (roasted marrow seeds), *iliosporous* (black sunflower seeds) and peanuts; ready packaged in paper bags with the price stamped on them. There is usually a man with his basket of *koulouria* (bread rings, like pretzels) crying 'Fresh Thessalonikis, beautiful koulouria Thessalonikis!' for 'Thessalonikis' are the best type of thicker rings with extra sesame seeds on top. Three-wheelers selling hot *bougatsa* (a sweet pastry made with cream, filo pastry, sugar and cinnamon), *loukoumades* (small doughnuts with dustings of cinnamon) an *spanakapittes* (spinach pies), regularly greet the early morning ferries out of Piraeus.

In Syros, the elegant capital of the Cyclades with its miniature copy of Milan's La Scala opera house, men in white jackets rush on to the ships to sell as much *loukoumia* (Turkish delight) and *halvadopitta* (circles of soft nougat and pistachio nuts sandwiched between layers of wafered pitta) as they can, returning to the backstreet factories to refill their baskets for the next arrival. People from the island come on laden with kilos of the excellent local *graviera* cheese bought from the *tiropoleon* (cheese shop) on the waterfront.

The Greeks are inveterate travellers and a family will usually take a picnic on the boats. Cold *keftedes* (meat balls) or *dolmades* (stuffed vine leaves), boiled eggs and cheese, always bread and fruit. But, for foreigners, dumped in the middle of the night amidst the low-life *souvlaki* stands and backstreet neon bars of Piraeus, their first introduction to Greek food may well be on the ferries the next day.

Ferry food, if nothing else, helps relieve the boredom of a long journey and offers some insight into the ways of the Greek kitchen. Dishes are cooked early and left to cool. The menus belong to a time when it was fashionable to serve semi-international style food.

These are dishes that are found on every Greek menu and have, over the years, lost any of their original sense through countless reprints and misspellings. *Bidok me avga* (a primitive hamburger with fried egg on top), *bon filet* (think of it as a 'steak') and *schnitzel* were once the modish dishes to eat but have now been debased into the culinary currency of the ferries.

The sit-down *schnitzel* has become the smart thing to eat on long voyages. Young men returning from military service treat themselves to this egg-battered piece of meat that bears no resemblance to its Viennese ancestry before eating some real home cooking again. Many never hear the brief garbled announcements for meal services on the boats and resort to the

standard snacks: dried-out pizzas, flaked-out *tiropittes* (cheese pies) and *tost* (toasted ham and cheese) in desperation.

The islands on the tourist trail can offer little better at times. Multi-lingual menus promise 'Greek specialities' like *moussaka*, *kebabs*, stuffed vine leaves (usually tinned), chops, chicken and the infamous summer Greek salad, *horiatiki* to its friends, a repetitive mess to its enemies forced to eat it on a daily basis. Fast food outlets proliferate and offer toasted sandwiches or rolls with any filling from *tzatziki* or Russian salad to *loukanika* (sausages) and cheese, made while the customers play video machines. There are *barakia* (small bars) in Ios and Santorini serving happy-hour cocktails like Greek Buck (Metaxa brandy, ouzo and lemon juice) and draught lager to an endless reggae beat, oblivious of the old woman trying to sleep next door. These establishments are in every side street in the Cyclades. They even advertise on the local FM radio station. 'Wild smooth tunes set a tone for something out of the ordinary . . . international cuisine. Hot food, curry and roast. Papagalos restaurant, Naxos. Only 60 m (65 yds) from the square.' Or, 'Bar Stella. Best breakfast, food, tropical cocktails. The only place everything can happen at Naoussa, Paros.'

It is not only the tourists that are to blame, for the young Greeks enjoy these places just as much when they are holiday. If they live away from home or are studying at university, they survive on a fast food diet like their role models, the American youth.

But some islands are different, either because they are off the daily ferry routes, like Kythera and Antikythera, Karpathos and Kassos, or because their size has enabled them to absorb visitors more easily. Large islands like Mitilini, Samos, Chios and even Rhodes with their many villages have kept traditions strong. Mytilini (or Lesbos as it is also known) has always maintained an arrogant aloofness from the rest of the Aegean. It has its own unique history and culture. Both Sappho, the sixth

Two volcanic islets, Nea and Palea Kameni, are active and sulphurous craters, visited daily by the tourist caiques from Santorini.

Three brothers just back from a fishing trip in Tilos, one of the smaller islands of the Dodecanese.

Right: Remote Kastellorizo harbour opposite Kas in Turkey.

century BC erotic poet and thinker, and Theophilos, the early twentieth-century primitive painter, were somewhat misunderstood in their time and died tragically, the former throwing herself off a rock for the love of a man, the latter in abject poverty, and both have been rehabilitated to almost cult status. Its highly developed literary and artistic traditions give its capital, Mytilini, a strange cosmopolitan air. In amongst the classic *ouzerie* with their excellent *mezedes* of *karavides* (prawns), *garides* (shrimps), salted *gavro* (anchovies) and freshly grilled *sardelles* (sardines), are the posters for the art movies and poetry readings performed throughout the summer season.

Perhaps its aloofness comes from its size and situation; it is the third largest island in the Aegean with a population of 90,000 in many scattered villages and lies nestled against the Turkish coast. Probably, it has more to do with the fact that tourism, although important, is not vital to the island economy.

Some of the best olives and olive oil come from the island's 11 million trees. There is a large canning industry based on the sardines and anchovies trapped annually in the Gulf of Kaloni and two dishes, popular throughout Greece, are made when anchovies are plentiful, *gavros sto fourno* (baked anchovies with garlic and herbs) and *gavros ladoxido* (pickled anchovies in oil and vinegar). *Sardelles pastes* (salted sardines) are also prepared for the winter months.

Ouzo is another old industry, based around the town of Plomari on the south coast. The Varvayannis distillery produces two of the best ouzos, a 'deluxe' blue-labelled bottle simply called 'Barbayannis' and the 'Aphrodite' brand, a favourite tourist buy with its kitsch label of neo-classical columns and armless statue. It bears the classic inscription: 'This rare liquor is pure ambrosia. Ancient history claims that this drink was partaken by the Gods, making them immortal.' Sometimes there are tours available, showing the distillation process with tastings.

Chios, east of Mytilini and even closer to the Turkish coast, is another wealthy island, based in the past on its merchants trading in silk, wines and mastic which can still be found in the spice markets of Istanbul and Cairo. *Mastika* the milky resin of the mastic tree, seems to be unique to the island and is still a vital cottage industry employing the women of the *Mastikochoria* – mastic villages – of the south. In the past, mastic was used by the Romans to clean their teeth and by the Ottoman sultans as a breath freshener. Today, it is still made into basic chewing gum and sold all over Greece, or smartly boxed for export to the Middle East where it is popular as a flavouring ingredient in many sweets and pastries. It is also used in the production of the local *mastika* liqueur. Large lumps look yellowish rock crystals and miraculously, when masticated, turn into a soft, flavourless chewing-gum.

In the mornings, the Chiot women of Mesta and Pirgi go by donkey to collect the resin from the mastic groves. With an old cloth at the base of the squat trees, they use a knife to scrape the resin 'tears' that come out of the bark on to the

cloth. At the factory, it is washed, drained and then pressed into chewing gum shapes or the larger pieces are drained and boxed for export. About 150 tons are produced every year at the costly price of about £60 a kilo.

Pirgi is the most unusual of the mastic villages. The houses display the accumulated wealth of the villagers in cunning black and white geometric designs known as *xysta*. Those not involved in the mastic collection are to be seen in the late summer stringing tomatoes. These are then hung from every balcony for use in the winter months for *pelte* (tomato sauce).

But other islands are reluctant to give away any secrets about their heritage. Having sold their souls to the devil, the locals feel a desperate need to keep some of their original identity to themselves. Perhaps most visitors are thought to be uninterested. It is frustrating to ask for local specialities when a glazed look comes over the fast-buck taverna owner who has just invested all his money in installing a self-service counter and plastic signs announcing 'English breakfast served here'. Having built up imported, second-hand notions about Paradise, it is hard to suddenly knock down the façade and offer the humble food eaten at home.

In remote Kastellorizo, or Megisti, the Easter celebrations can be enjoyed by anyone who makes the effort to go there. This tiny island welcomes all visitors with a proud sign proclaiming the fact that it is Europe's final frontier. The last Aegean island in effect, seventy miles (112 km) east of Rhodes or an eight-hour journey once or twice a week on an aged ferry called The *Panormitis*. There is a landing strip now and flights from Rhodes by light aircraft (but these are heavily booked in summer and at

Rock flowers (left) and wild artichokes (right) bring colour and food to the island at Easter time.

Easter) and a small military base, for the island is a mile away from the Turkish coast and the thriving tourist town of Kas. One of the largest flags in the Aegean flies defiantly atop the ruined crusader castle and from the neighbouring island of Ro. Now uninhabited, an old woman, known throughout Greece as *I kyra tis Ro* (the woman of Ro) used to live there alone until her death a few years ago and kept it as Greek soil by hoisting the flag every day.

At Easter, the Aegean island undergoes a dramatic transformation. Even a barren island like Kastellorizo, bursts into flower. There are marguerites and poppies, purple sage and fennel on most available flat ground and on the paths up to the island's plateau and the church of Aghios Ioannis, horseshoe orchids and lilac crocuses flourish. There are also vegetable plots for there is no room in the cramped port and capital for any serious gardens except the omnipresent flower pots and basil plants in courtyards. These vegetable plots are filled with lettuces, artichokes, celery, fresh garlic and spring onions (scallions), herbs like parsley, mint and dill. If it has rained, there will be secret caches of *sparangia* (wild asparagus) in the mountainous ravines.

On *Kathari Deftera*, or Clean Monday, the first fasting day of Lent, the bakery sells *lagana*, a special unleavened bread and the islanders begin the fast with a typical meal of boiled octopus with oil and vinegar, *taramosalata* and *halva* (crushed sesame seeds).

For the next forty days, the faithful then eat *Sarakostiana* or lenten fasting food. This means no meat or poultry, dairy products or fresh fish. Vegetables, pulses, olives, bloodless crustaceans like prawns or shellfish like clams and mussels, octopus and squid can be eaten. The effect on an island like Kastellorizo is not great for their diet is mostly based on the sea supplemented by seasonal vegetables and dried pulses.

The once thriving island becomes alive again as Holy Week approaches and the exiles return from Athens or Rhodes with carefully tied cardboard boxes, gifts for family and friends; a new colour television set for aged parents, a cassette player for a younger brother.

During the Second World War, when the island was evacuated after the British bombed and destroyed many of the fine sea captains' houses around the quay, most of the populace were evacuated to Palestine or Egypt, never to return, settling mostly in Perth, Australia. It is only in the last ten years that the island has suddenly become a place of homage for the retired and a new generation of Australian Greeks who think of it as home. They have brought a new prosperity back to the island, money to restore the bombed buildings again and work to those that remain. The Greek government is also anxious for the island to show signs of life again after its slow death in the last three decades and gave the money for one of the best museums in the Aegean.

Kastellorizo was once a rich sea-trading island full of merchant ships that plied the routes from the Dodecanese to the Levant, Cyprus and Alexandria in Egypt until the advent of steam power destroyed the livelihoods of many old merchant families around the Aegean. Today there is still one of the most beautiful caiques in Greece, built by a famous Athenian boat-builder Psaros, called *Alkmini*, that now belongs to Yourgos, the owner of the Little Paris taverna on the waterfront. Moored outside the taverna, it stands with its unused sail as a grim reminder of past glories. This is one of the most perfect places to eat fresh fish in Greece. The tables are so close to the water that people often exuberantly lean back on their chairs and fall in. The food is standard taverna fare, including grilled fish like *skoumbri* (mackerel), *kynigos* (dolphin fish) or *mayatico* (amberjack) when in season. In the shallow waters by the quay, Yourgos will bring out a huge trident and spear *soupies* (cuttlefish) or octopus in the early evening.

It is the *parea* or crowd of friends that is always at this taverna that matters. No one passes by the tables without being offered a glass or

The priest and his drinking partners at the Little Paris taverna in Kastellorizo.

discussed in irreverent tones. After food and drink, gossip seems the next most important thing. The priest of the island, a legendary hell-raiser known throughout the Dodecanese for his mad antics, sits with Yourgos plotting their latest trick. Often, they will suddenly take off in the caique and go fishing for a few hours, with their bottle of wine and packets of cigarettes, maybe even a few tourists for company with the promise of seeing the cave of Perasta, nicknamed the 'Blue Grotto'. This is well worth the visit, crouched in a rowing boat under the small opening, the cave opens up into a chamber that is about 70 ft (21.5 m) high. There are stalactites and sometimes seals, but the wonder is the emerald colour of the water if caught at the right time when the rising sun's rays filter through the narrow entrance.

The preparations for Easter begin properly on Maundy Thursday when the women of the island bake special biscuits and cakes like *koulourakia* (hand-rolled biscuits) and *tsoureki* (braided sweet bread with a red egg in the middle). Children are dispatched to the shops to buy red dye for the easter eggs. *Kokkina avga* (red eggs) are made by adding the dye to boiling water and vinegar; the eggs are cleaned, dried and then boiled in this mixture for 10 minutes. Afterwards, they are left to cool, dried again and polished with olive oil to bring out the shine.

The families of the island prepare Easter cakes. Far right: Koulourakia biscuits just out of the oven.

The traditional Easter game of *tsougrisma*, similar to conkers, is played by everyone on Easter Sunday. Bowls of eggs are placed on dining tables and offered to every guest. One person holds an egg out for an opponent to tap; the one that cracks is eaten by the loser while the victorious egg plays on.

The baker has been busy making *lazaropsomo* – bread with currants and sesame seeds – and *prosforo* (holy bread) stamped with the church seal. The men begin to slaughter lambs or goats and the children go out for walks in search of wild flowers to decorate the church with on Good Friday.

For once, the priest leaves his waterfront table and works like a man possessed. It is the one time of year when he can redeem himself and with all the island watching his every move, he puts on the performance some priests only ever dream about.

Good Friday is a day of rest and total fasting. In the square above the port, opposite the main church of Agios Constantinos, a taverna serves *revitho-keftedes* (chick-pea rissoles), *fava* (split-pea purée) and *fakes* (lentil soup), typical fasting food for the foreign visitors. The church is still decorated with *vaya* – palms woven into crosses – from the Palm Sunday

service the week beofre as the children cover the *epitaphio* (funeral bier) with flowers, often violets, in preparation for the evening procession. Slowly, the church fills in time for the procession. Lemon and orange blossom struggles against the smell of smoking candles and overpowering incense as the priest sprinkles rose water over the congregation. At about 9pm, the funeral procession, re-enacting the burial of Christ, begins. The priest leaves the church, accompanied by some of the older children carrying the cross and banners, followed by the bier, for the square. The islanders then jostle for a place behind the local dignitaries, the mayor and doctor, the captain of the military base and a retired admiral who comes every year, leading the procession around the narrow streets and back again to the church, where the bier is laid to rest in the sanctuary behind the altar screen.

It is the evening service the next day, on Holy Saturday, that is the most eagerly awaited; everyone makes the effort to attend the climax of the Greek religious Easter. Soldiers from the base, glad to break the monotony of pointless military service, come to the square and stand self-consciously around the edges of the crowd in their pressed uniforms and short haircuts.

has risen) and reply 'Alithos Anesti' (Truly he has risen), and wish each other a happy Easter.

Some people stay until the mass ends in the early hours but most rush home to break the long fast with the traditional Easter soup, *mayeritsa*, made from the intestines, heart and lungs of the paschal lamb. This is a meal of great importance. The family, weary after the service, eat quietly before going to bed. Red eggs are cracked and eaten, the bread is torn fervently as lemon juice is squeezed into the soup bowls and the fast is symbolically broken. Not everyone can be bothered nowadays to make *mayeritsa* with its laborious cleaning of the intestines but, when properly made, with chopped spring onions (scallions), celery and parsley leaves, dill and *avgolemono* (the sauce made from beaten eggs, lemon juice and the soup stock), it is a classic Greek dish of great intensity.

The real celebration begins on Easter Sunday with the lunchtime family feast. If the weather is good, the harbour-front tavernas and houses are emptied of tables and chairs, which are set up outside. Tables are joined together and covered with linen tablecloths in private homes or throw-away paper ones in the tavernas. Lemons are cut and quartered in bowls along the table, green salads with chopped spring onions (scallions) and dill and dishes of olives are also placed at regular intervals for all to reach. There are plates of *lakerda* (pickled chunks of bonito or tuna) and bowls of *tzatziki* (yoghurt and garlic dip) on some large tables to keep the impatient happy. Bread, bottles of red wine and *kokkina avga* are also plentiful. Some families and tavernas spit-roast their lamb over charcoal, others still use the bakery and take their *tapsia*, the large round tins used for *sto fourno* (oven cooking) early in the morning for the slow bake that gives the meat such a delicious flavour. Potatoes are placed around the meat and cooked in its juices with the addition of a little water, lemon juice and dried herbs like oregano or thyme. Sometimes, a simple stuffing is also made with chopped liver, onion, dill, bread and lemon

Easter celebrations culminate with the mass on Holy Saturday when at midnight the congregation gathers outside the church.

One of the policemen of the island, usually to be seen in his designer track-suit and running shoes in pursuit of tourist girls (*kamaki*), has waxed his moustache and polished his boots. Everyone is dressed in their best clothes, smelling of cheap cologne and hairspray.

For the final part of the long service, people crowd into the church holding white candles – the children's are decorated with red ribbons and gold thread – which they try to light from the priest's candle or from someone close to him. At midnight, the church bells ring and fireworks are let off as everyone greets each other with the statement 'Christos Anesti' (Christ

After preparing the paschal lamb at home the villagers gather outside the oven which the baker then carefully fills with the individual dishes.

juice. Everywhere there is a sense of anticipation and excitement as the appointed hour approaches. At the bakery, the women are nervously gossiping. 'Open the oven before our husbands kill us', one of them cries. As the sweating baker hauls the *tapsia* out of his oven, the aromas of roast lamb or goat with mountain herbs are intoxicating. After they have compared each other's efforts, they return triumphantly to the tables.

When the meat arrives, there are cheers from the tables around the harbour and glasses clink with the toast 'kali orexsi' ('bon appetit'). By late afternoon, people begin to meander from table to table, always drinking and eating a plate of food when offered. Some people need siestas, others carry on until the evening when the island party or *glenti* begins.

This is held in the village hall opposite Agios Constantinos in the square above the port. A circular dance-floor has been cleared around the musicians with their small loudspeakers. They have a long night ahead of them and are tuning their instruments – violin, lute and *bouzouki* – calmly. The longer they play, the more money they are likely to make as dancers put banknotes on the loudspeakers or throw them exuberantly at their feet; making their jouney from Rhodes all

the more worthwhile.

By 10pm, the long tables are filling with the islanders. Beer is the most popular drink, consumed in huge quantities as people begin sending bottles from table to table. Everyone brings their own *mezedes*, cold lamb and potatoes, salad and cheese. An elderly couple begin the dancing, the young need more to drink before they start the serious business of asking girls to dance especially when their mothers are counting the number of times prospective suitors are up on the dance-floor.

Outside, more crates of beer are soon being packed into the fridges and the taverna opposite is frying plate after plate of chips brought over on large wooden trays. By 3am, almost everyone has been dancing wildly, drunkenly clapping and shouting to each other. An English tourist girl is dancing with a soldier for the third time, unaware of the merriment she is causing the rest of the room. Outside, the wind is rising and the stars are clear. If anyone were to arrive from Turkey, there would be nobody in the port, the elderly asleep and the rest of the island still celebrating till dawn.

Two days later, the ferry arrives to take the visitors back home to Athens and Australia. There are last drinks and tearful farewells when

Right: A roadside Ikonostassi (shrine) set amongst the orange groves behind Chania.

Cleaning entrails for mayeritsa soup in Kastellorizo.

it is time to leave. In a moment of madness, the priest jumps on to *Alkmini* and lets off a flare as the *Panormitis* departs. 'You'll start a war with Turkey', scolds the policeman, unable to do anything with the man that made Easter so memorable.

The island resumes normal life again until the summer. Yourgos is counting his takings after the rush and the blind man's *periptero* is quiet, there are no confusing voices for him anymore. The baker has received more flour off the ferry and is loading the sacks on to his donkey, as always sweating in his white vest. The rest of the island is getting ready to fish for there is nothing else to do on this very barren, typically Greek island.

A mile across the water, in Kas, the Muslim call to prayer from the *muezzin* is an insistent echo. The carpet and trinket shops are also waiting for the summer tourists. The *dolmus* buses outside the market take villagers back to their mountain homes, laden with fresh vegetables and fruit. The richness of Turkey's Mediterranean coastal plains could not be more different from the apparent poverty of Kastellorizo but there is always the old Turk who speaks Greek and asks for cigarettes who looks nostalgically across the water.

The Dodecanese and Ionian islands more readily show the influences of the various occupations by the Venetian, modern Italian and Ottoman empires. It is reflected in their architecture, language and, to some extent, their cuisine. Corfu, especially, has managed to preserve some of the sophistication that 400 years under the Venetians (1386–1797) ingrained into its everyday cooking. When the rest of Greece was under Ottoman rule and began to absorb elements of Turkish cuisine, Corfu prospered under Venetian rule. They ate more pasta and cured meats like the Italians and used less spices and olive oil than mainland Greece. There are three dishes that are Corfu's unique contribution to the Greek kitchen. *Sofrito* (braised veal with a wine vinegar sauce), *bourtheto* (fish casserole) and *pastitsada* (baked veal with spaghetti). All show their Venetian ancestry, *sofrito* in its use of wine and vinegar, *bourtheto* with its use of cayenne pepper (a legacy of the Venetian spice trade) and *pastitsada* in its vital ingredient – thick spaghetti. All three have been adopted into the repertoire of mainland restaurants.

There is one island more than any other that has a life of its own. Crete's proud heritage survives through its literature, music, dress, dialect and a cuisine that mirrors both the fecundity of its lowlands and its wild mountains. After years of dominant, oppressive rule by the Venetians and Turks, it has retained a fierce independence, a curious synthesis of all that is Greek today.

In late autumn, towards the end of November, after most of the tourist hotels and bars have

Previous pages: *Chania market at sunset.*

been closed along the deserted beaches of the island's long coastline, the olive harvest begins and carries on relentlessly until mid-winter. In western Crete, olive trees and orange groves line the roads towards the mountain valleys. Beyond Chania the road to the mountain plain of Omalos, from where the descent to the Samaria Gorge begins, passes through citrus groves of orange, mandarin and grapefruit, always snaking upwards to the Lefka Ori, or White Mountains. This snow-capped range dominates the landscape, home to hunted freedom fighters in various wars.

Today, the migrant shepherds and their flocks roam the upper reaches, inexperienced walkers arrive in coaches to tackle the lower reaches of the Samaria Gorge, Europe's longest ravine that trickles out to the east coast at Agia Roumeli. Wild herbs and medicinal plants also grow on the slopes and are picked by the mountain villagers to be sold in Chania market or to the makers of Campari, the Italian bitter aperitif with its secret recipe of herbs and spices.

There is a new road at the far end of the plain, hacked into the mountainside that zigzags downwards, past flocks of sheep and hooded crows, a desolate landscape of straggled pines, twisted out of shape by the wind. At Prasses and Sempronas, two villages famous for their chestnut trees, the leaves are falling into small streams, the colours of autumn decomposing slowly in the shallow water. A woman is selling large red apples from her orchard, another is walking her goats through a field, shouting and waving with her stick as they continually stop to pick at the low branches of the trees.

There are black nets or large sheets of plastic laid underneath the olive trees as the road comes back to the fertile region around Chania. *Throumbes*, the ripe black olives that fall from

Baskets of windfallen olives.

Far right: *Sifting olives during the autumn harvest.*

the trees and dry in the wind, are picked by families, crouching with their *kalathi* (baskets). These shrivelled olives are sold in markets (as are ripe olives for people who do not have their own trees) and if preserved in salt they can keep up to five years.

In the small village of Malaxa, which looks down on Souda bay, the *kafeneion* called 'Paradise' is empty save for its old and blind owner. He sits outside the brightly painted door and sign. 'Everyone is in the fields today', he sighs, unable to join them, lost in his solitary world of village sounds, the wind, the church bells and his dog that barks whenever a customer approaches.

On one plot of land, an elderly couple, Pandelis and Maria, are struggling with their trees. 'When I was young I could do seven or eight trees in a day but now it's hard to do even three', reminisces Pandelis as he sits resting on one of the large sacks already brimming with green olives. The trees are young ten-year-olds that yield 5 kilos (11 lb) of olives and 1 kilo (2 lb) of olive oil. But they still need to be cut and pruned and he is soon up in the branches again, beating them with his *dembli*, the special stick used to shake the olive tree. Large branches are cut and later stripped of their olives and leaves. The olives and leaves beaten down on to the nets are then winnowed like corn, thrown up into the air to separate the leaves from the olives. His wife is also working with a stand and wire-mesh frame, shaking the frame to push the olives on to the netting below.

In the modern olive press, the trucks and donkeys are bringing the sacks to be pressed. There is the unmistakable harsh smell of the processing which nobody seems to mind; it is the smell of survival. The olive oil is the lifeblood of the kitchen, indispensable to all cooking and contributes to the healthy, low cholesterol diets of the Greeks, especially in the remote villages where eating habits remain unaffected by new dietary trends. The residue from the mill makes pure olive oil soap and

pirina, the peat-like fuel made from crushed stones. Those that produce a surplus give the oil away to family and friends, keeping land and traditions alive in this simple product of the fields.

Much that is cultivated around western Crete ends up in Chanta market or in container ships bound for the rest of Europe. Chanta's market is one of the most orderly and clean in Greece. A cast-iron cruciform building based on Marseilles market opens early in the morning when the traders and truck-drivers sit down to eat and drink in the small tavernas around the market. Inside, where the fish stalls begin, there is one taverna that does the best business. A gypsy family who have brought their produce down to sell are eating a celebratory breakfast of sheep's head, fried *kolokthia* – courgettes (zucchini) – and a kilo *kandari* (the meal measuring jug used in all tavernas) of red wine. Opposite, there is another smaller taverna specializing in *patsa* (tripe soup), always eaten by ravenous market traders all over Greece. The fishmongers beckon to their stalls, each decorated in inimitable fashion. One has a beautiful sign, a primitive painting of an enduring image of the Aegean, a girl riding a fish with caiques and fishermen in the background; another with a sense of humour, puts a carnation in the mouth of a large and ugly *rophos* (grouper). Outside this section of the market, there is a large *kafeneon* where the men sit with their *metrio* coffee or herbal teas like *faskomilo* (sage) which is good for colds.

On the other side are the dairy shops. Some sell only the thick yoghurt in earthenware bowls and *staka*, a soft white cream cheese used in a local dish also of that name, when it is combined with eggs and baked or fried. Both come from Vrises, a village on the way to Rethymnon where a taverna specializes in the dish. The tables underneath a large plane tree, next to a small trickle of a river, where the owner serves strong local red wine and crusty bread to mop up the plates of *staka*. The best *staka* used to come from water buffalo's milk, when that animal was

Some of the colourful fresh produce sold at the stalls of Chania market.

common in northern Greece but now it is made when the sheep are nursing their young.

The cheese shops are just as artistic. One of the owners, in traditional Cretan black costume of riding boots and breeches, cummerbund, waistcoat and turban fringed with beads, is piling the cheeses into pyramids. *Graviera* (which tastes like Gruyère), *kopanisti* (a blue cheese), *kefalotiri* (the yellowish, hard cheese used for grating) and *anthotiri* (a moulded, hard *mizithra* – goats cheese) are the most popular.

Each fruit and vegetable stall sells different-sized baskets hanging from ropes, surrounded by strings of fragile persimmons, onions and garlic. There are all types of *horta* (wild greens) available, depending on the season from *vrouves* (charlock or field mustard) *radikia* (dandelion leaves) to high-priced leaves used sparsely in *hortopittes* (pies), radishes, red cabbages and the omni-present potato. *Mousmoulo* (medlars), *fragosika* (prickly pear), *kidonia* (quince), and *rodia* (pomegranate) are all fruits that grow in abundance in the temperate winter climate. The herb and nut stall owners are used to foreigners buying mountain herbs for cooking and medicinal purposes. Many are packaged especially for them. Cretan saffron, *dictamo* (dittany) used to make tea, cummin, *dafni* (bay leaves), *dendroli-*

vano (rosemary) and then all the medicinal herbs like *lagodohorto* or *chrissohorto* said to be good for the stomach and heart. Whatever the ailment, there will be a Cretan cure.

Down past the *souvlaki* fast-food joints and hippy cafés, in the backstreets of the Venetian harbour, are the late-night disco bars that keep the US navy base happy. Nobody drinks ouzo or locally made *raki* (also called *tsikoudia*), it is beer and bourbon and the sound of honky tonk and other red-neck rock is played out of season. Then they have all the atmosphere of the middle American bar-room. Faded dollar bills pinned up and naval insignia ripped off uniforms on the first night of shore leave. The locals don't care for they are big business however unpopular the US bases are politically for most Greeks.

Beyond these bars, close to the Venetian armouries in the old harbour walls, are two fish tavernas, called Logari and Chanion, where the fishermen and locals eat. They serve *kalamarakia* (fried squid), *barbounia* shredded cabbage and *horta* salads like *patsaria me skordalia* (beetroot with garlic sauce) in the winter months when everyone crowds inside, exhausted after a day's work in the olive groves.

The road to Therissos leads past the faded ochre Venetian farmhouses with their courtyards

Left: *One of the popular cheese shops in Chania market.*

Making a Cretan speciality,
Skaltsounia *(small cheese or horta*
pies) over the fire in Therissos.

Right: Around Prasses, the
landscape is dominated by
chestnut and apple trees.

more comfortable houses in the suburbs of Chania.

Those that remain in the shadow of the Lefka Ori, live on in two-storey houses with the fire-wood stacked under eaves and chickens wandering beneath the chestnut trees. An old couple live in the last house of the village. It is one of those rare houses, sometimes encountered in rural Greece, in complete harmony with its surroundings.

Despite the hardships of winter life, the couple who live there remain in close contact with the mountain and its seasons. It is a house of noble poverty. Wooden stairs lead up to the second floor bedroom, dominated by a cast-iron bed and sacks of nuts: *kastana* (chestnuts), almonds and *foundoukia* (hazelnuts). The huge fireplace, with its craggy contours smeared with the smoke and flame stains from the fire that seem to take the shape of primitive cave paintings, dominates downstairs. In the dim light of the fire, the old woman sits on a small rock seat that surrounds the fire, boiling the roots and leaves of a wild plant that she picked in the foothills. Her husband is whittling away at a shepherd's crook with his hunting knife, scraping the hard wood into shape.

Inside the fireplace hang saucepans and onions and a small bamboo tube that she blows to bring the fire to life. Strings of *bournelodo-mates* (plum tomatoes) crowd the rafters and crude, faded newspaper, cut out to look like the usual diamond shapes of kitchen embroidery, overhangs the mantelpiece. While he drinks a glass of warming *tsikoudia* with some nuts, she is preparing *skaltsounia*. These are small Cretan pies, made with wild *horta* or goats cheese and fresh herbs. A simple pastry is prepared with flour, water and olive oil to which she adds cheese and herbs; these are fried in a shallow saucepan until they turn a golden colour. The couple eat outside, beneath a chestnut tree, staring up at the mountains above them. Perhaps they are thinking about their family far away in Athens and America who visit them every year.

and wells, many now owned by experimental farmers who have planted lychee plants amidst the banana and orange trees. At one farm, called 'Bella Campagna', the overloaded avocado trees stoop into the road waiting to be picked. The village of Therissos is reached through a narrow gorge and was famous as the place where Eleftherios Venizelos, one of the founders of modern Greece, held an outlawed assembly in 1905 in favour of union with the mainland. Like the monastery of Arkadi, where hundreds of Cretans were blown up when the Turks attacked it in 1866, it is a pilgrimage for many people. But it has a sad, dilapidated feel to it; of desertion to

The blind owner of the Paradise kafeneion in *Malaxa.*

Left: The amphora and pots on sale here are used for storing grains and olive oil.

Nothing would make them leave this village where they are at peace with their world; offering the famed Cretan *philoxenia* (hospitality) to passers-by. A bag full of nuts, a glass of *tsikoudia* and if he takes a particular liking to someone, one of his cherished shepherd's crooks.

If this is the acceptable face of rural Crete, Rethymnon is the ideal country market town and port. A curious mixture of Venetian arches and doorways mixed with typical wooden Turkish balconies. The main market street is full of small crowded shops, the owners sitting outside on wooden boxes, talking to one another. A widow is stripping the leaves from long spindly radishes opposite a barbershop window filled with Cretan knives with horn handles. Near the stone arch entrance to the town, an old bakery sells good bread and *paximadia*, dried rusks with anise, another Cretan speciality. A large vegetable stall sells cultivated *manitaraia*

(mushrooms) and baskets of *salingaria* (snails) which the Greeks love. In Crete, the snails are a favourite food often cooked with *horta, stafides* (raisins), tomatoes or *pligouri* (cracked wheat). They are caught after it has rained, the hills dotted with crouched figures collecting among the shrubs and bushes. Then, they are purged by being fed on wheat, flour and herbs for a few days before a final day of fasting when they are ready to cook.

Past the locked doors of the mosque and its fluted minaret, close to the Rimondi Fountain (built in 1629) with its three lions' head spouts and Corinthian columns, is Paleologos Street. A family-run butcher's shop is busy selling *kouneli* (rabbit) for the favourite winter stew of *stifado* (the meat is slow cooked with shallots and vinegar), pig's heads to make *pikti* (jellied pork) and cuts of mountain-reared lamb. A man sells *hamoures*, the wind-dried, newly fallen olives;

trachana dried crushed wheat and soured goat's milk which makes a thick soup, is fried or dunked into glasses of hot milk, *stragalia* (roasted chick-peas) and local honey. Next door, there is a hardware store with new rope for the caiques, home-made olive oil soap and sturdy baskets. A *zacharoplasteon* cake shop carries on the good tradition that the town has for cakes and sweets, selling *galaktoboureko*, *poutinga*, *kataifi*, raisins and small mandarins in syrup. A canary yellow *periptero* (kiosk) advertises the Hollywood action at the local cinema in a sign hammered into the eucalyptus tree. The whole street has something of the air of London's Portobello Road, especially in the summer when it is crowded with tourists on their way down to the old harbour with its fish tavernas and fishing boats, set three course meals of *taramosalata*, fried *kalamaria* and *xiphias*, bottles of retsina drunk at the outside tables, perched at the waters edge, where Mammon meets Dionysus. Behind, the maze of narrow streets are reminiscent of the gloomy alleys of Venice in winter.

Iraklion, Crete's ugly capital has only one redeeming feature, the backstreet *ouzeries* and *kafeneia* in the centre. One of them, called 'O Collegio', surrounded by the video rental shops (which are sweeping like a plague through the modern Greek city) and tourist boutiques, is a last meeting place for a few locals who like the old ways of country living. The owner makes it his business to keep his customers happy with a bewildering variety of wild *horta* for *mezedes*.

Served with carafes of *raki*, in this basic taverna of vivid pink and blue walls, rickety tables and rush chairs, the wild *horta* finds as appreciative an audience as one that is tasting different vintages of some fine wine. Waxy, yellow potatoes are baked slowly in the oven and when served, the owner makes a great display of cutting them in half and sprinkling them with sea salt and lemon juice. Small salads are finely shredded out of a huge white cabbage with an ornately inscribed shepherd's knife. Plates of small shrivelled black olives are mixed with a sliced tomato, sweet-tasting onions are quartered with strips of cucumber. As the old men wander in, they give the owner plastic bags tightly packed with *horta* for him to prepare. Wild plants and flowers are eaten raw or boiled, some even fried in batter like courgette (zucchini) flowers. Untranslatable bounty from the hills like *stamnagathi* and *mandalides* are what a Cretan appreciates. Tonight, the owner serves thin stalks of *sparangi* (wild asparagus) and emerald-green sheaths of *papoules* (sweet pea shoots) eaten raw with salt and vinegar. After a few carafes of *raki*, retired sea-captains and shepherds will begin to retell their wartime stories of freedom fighters and ambushes in the mountain ranges of the island.

Avgolemono

Egg-lemon sauce

This indispensable Greek sauce, which is added to soups and stews, needs concentration from the cook and a low heat, if it is not to curdle. Restaurant chefs use only the yolks with added cornflour (cornstarch). Some cooks beat the yolk and whites separately.

SERVES 4
2 eggs
juice of 1-2 lemons
75 ml/5 tbsp hot stock

Beat the eggs for 3 minutes, then beat in the lemon juice. Slowly add the hot (never boiling or the eggs will curdle) stock, beating the mixture all the time.

If the sauce is to be added back to a stew, it is now whisked in. If it is to be served separately as a sauce for boiled or baked fish dishes, place the bowl over a saucepan of simmering water, without letting the bowl come into contact with the water (or use a double boiler), and whisk until the sauce thickens.

Faki

Lentil soup

SERVES 4-6
450 g/1 lb/2⅔ cups lentils
1 large onion, coarsely chopped
75-90 ml/5-6 tbsp olive oil
2-3 garlic cloves, finely chopped
2 bay leaves
salt and freshly ground black pepper
1.75 litres/3 pints/7½ cups water
15 ml/1 tbsp red wine vinegar

Wash the lentils and drain. In a large saucepan, gently fry the onion in 30 ml/2 tbsp olive oil for 2 minutes. Then add the garlic, bay leaves, salt and pepper to taste and the water and simmer the lentils gently for 30-40 minutes, skimming the surface of froth if necessary. During cooking, add the rest of the olive oil and more water if needed.

Just before serving, stir the vinegar into the soup. Serve with more vinegar at the table for those who want it.

Fava

Split-pea purée

SERVES 4-6
350 g/12 oz/1⅔ cups split-peas
2.5 litres/4 pints/2 quarts water
1 large onion, coarsely chopped
75-90 ml/5-6 tbsp olive oil
salt and freshly ground black pepper
For garnish:
1 onion, finely sliced
30-45 ml/2-3 tbsp olive oil
2 lemons, quartered

Wash the split-peas and put in a large saucepan. Add the water and bring to the boil, skimming the froth off with a spoon. When the water is clear, add the onion and olive oil and simmer uncovered for 2½ hours or until the split-peas are almost puréed. Allow to cool, then mash to purée consistency if necessary, season to taste and refrigerate.

When ready to serve, add sliced onion on top and dribble olive oil over the dish. Serve with lemons to squeeze over the *fava*.

Right: Fava, *split-pea puree.*

Mayeritsa

Easter 'midnight' soup

Traditionally made with the intestines of the Paschal lamb, this soup can use lamb meat to make a stock; it is also less bother.

SERVES 6

700-900 g/1½-2 lb leg or shoulder of lamb on the bone
900 g/2 lb lamb's offal – liver, heart and intestines (optional)
45 ml/3 tbsp finely chopped fresh dill
15 ml/1 tbsp finely chopped fresh flat-leafed parsley
15 ml/1 tbsp finely chopped celery tops
6 spring onions (scallions), including stems, chopped
1.2 litres/2 pints/5 cups water
45 g/1½ oz/3 tbsp butter
1 cos (romaine) lettuce heart, shredded finely
150 g/5 oz/¾ cup long-grain rice
salt and freshly ground black pepper
2 eggs, beaten,
juice of 1 lemon

Wash the meat and offal well, bone as necessary and cut into cubes. Place the meat in a saucepan with some of the herbs, 3 spring onions (scallions) and the water. Bring to the boil, skimming the froth off the surface. Cover and simmer for 45 minutes.

Sauté the remaining spring onions (scallions) in the butter. Take the meat out of the stock and add to the onions. Strain the stock and set aside. Add the offal, lettuce, remaining herbs, rice and seasoning to taste. Pour the stock over, with extra water if needed to cover the ingredients, and simmer until the rice is cooked.

Remove from the heat. Make an *avgolemono* sauce with some of the stock, the eggs and lemon juice (see page 80) and stir into the soup. Serve immediately.

Skaltsounia

Cretan pies

Every Cretan varies the ingredients for these pies according to the season. Generally, they are either savoury (with cheese or *horta*) or sweet, with soft *mezithra* cheese, nuts and cinnamon. They can be baked or fried.

SERVES 4

150 g/5 oz *feta* cheese, crumbled
1 medium-sized onion, finely diced, or 4 spring onions (scallions), chopped
1 egg, beaten
30 ml/2 tbsp finely chopped fresh mint
15 ml/1 tbsp finely chopped fresh flat-leafed parsley
salt and freshly ground black pepper
45 ml/3 tbsp olive oil for frying
For pastry:
225 g/8 oz/1⅔ cups plain (all-purpose) flour
pinch of salt
15 ml/1 tbsp olive oil
60 ml/4 tbsp water

To make the pastry, mix the flour, salt, oil and water in a bowl and knead into a soft dough. Cover and let it rest.

Mix the filling ingredients together in another bowl. Roll the dough out thinly and cut into 12.5 cm/5 inch diameter rounds. Add 30 ml/2 tbsp of filling to each round and fold over into half-moon shapes.

Heat the olive oil in a large, heavy frying pan and fry the pies until golden brown (about 2 minutes on each side).

Domates Gemistes

Stuffed tomatoes

One of the most familiar summer dishes, usually a mixture of tomatoes and green sweet peppers are stuffed with either a meat and rice or vegetable and rice stuffing. Large juicy Mediterranean tomatoes are crucial to the success of this dish.

SERVES 4
8 large tomatoes
salt and freshly ground black pepper
10 ml/2 tsp sugar
75-90 ml/5-6 tbsp olive oil
2 large onions, finely chopped
30 ml/2 tbsp finely chopped fresh mint
15 ml/1 tbsp finely chopped fresh flat-leafed parsley
30 ml/2 tbsp pine nuts (optional)
150 g/5 oz/¾ cup long-grain rice
30 ml/2 tbsp sultanas (golden raisins) (optional)
30 ml/2 tbsp tomato paste, dissolved in 150 ml/¼ pint/⅔ cup water

Preheat the oven to 180°C/350°F/Gas Mark 4.

Wash the tomatoes, slice off the tops (reserve them) and scoop out the flesh using a teaspoon, being careful not to break the skins. Set the flesh to one side. Sprinkle the insides with salt and sugar and set aside.

Heat 45 ml/3 tbsp oil in a frying pan and sauté the onions for 5 minutes. Then add the tomato pulp, herbs, seasoning and nuts (if using). Cook for a further 10 minutes and then add the rice and sultanas (golden raisins) and cook for another 5 minutes.

Rinse the tomatoes, then fill with the rice mixture and replace the tomato tops. Place in a baking tin. Pour the remaining olive oil and paste mixture around the tomatoes. Bake for 40 minutes. Best served lukewarm.

Gemista

Easter stuffing island style

SERVES 6
1 small loaf white bread
225 g/8 oz lamb's liver, washed and diced
4-5 spring onions (scallions), including stems, diced
30-45 ml/2-3 tbsp finely chopped fresh flat-leafed parsley
30-45 ml/2-3 tbsp finely chopped celery leaves
45 ml/3 tbsp finely chopped fresh dill
juice of 1 lemon
30 ml/2 tbsp finely chopped fresh mint
salt and freshly ground black pepper

Remove crusts from the bread, soak in a bowl of water for 10 minutes and then squeeze out the excess moisture. Combine all the ingredients together in a bowl and mix well.

In the islands this will be stuffed and sewn into the lamb before cooking; use a boned leg or shoulder of lamb for cooking this way. Otherwise, place the stuffing, with a covering of foil, in an ovenproof dish and bake alongside the lamb.

Kokkina Avga

Red Easter eggs

12 eggs
1 packet red dye (available from Greek food shops)
75-90 ml/5-6 tbsp red wine vinegar
1.2 litres/2 pints/5 cups water
olive oil

Wash and dry the eggs. Dissolve the dye in the vinegar. Bring the water to the boil in an old saucepan (the dye can stain the metal), add the vinegar-dye mix and continue boiling for a few minutes. Lower the eggs carefully into the saucepan and boil for 10 minutes, making sure they are completely covered in the solution. Plunge them into cold water, drain and dry. Polish with a little olive oil to make them shine.

Revitho-Keftedes

Chick-pea rissoles

SERVES 4-6
350 g/12 oz/1⅔ cups dried chick-peas
1.2 litres/2 pints/5 cups water
1 large potato, peeled and boiled
1 medium-sized onion, finely chopped
salt and freshly ground black pepper
30 ml/2 tbsp finely chopped fresh flat-leafed parsley
1 egg, beaten
30 ml/2 tbsp flour
30-45 ml/2-3 tbsp olive oil
1 lemon, quartered

Soak the chick-peas overnight in cold water. Drain and rinse then put in a pan with the measured fresh water and bring to the boil.

Simmer for 1½ hours or until soft. Drain.

Add the potato and onion. Mash the mixture, then add the seasoning, parsley and beaten egg. Shape into small rissoles (cakes).

Roll in the flour and fry in olive oil until golden brown on both sides. Serve with lemon quarters.

Lagos Stifado

Hare stew

SERVES 6
1 hare or rabbit, jointed (cut up)
60-75 ml/4-5 tbsp red wine
45-60 ml/3-4 tbsp red wine vinegar
2 garlic cloves, finely sliced
2 bay leaves
7.5 ml/½ tbsp black peppercorns
1 cinnamon stick
5 ml/1 tsp allspice berries (optional)
60-75 ml/4-5 tbsp olive oil
700 g/1½ lb shallots, peeled
15 ml/1 tbsp tomato paste, dissolved in 175 ml/6 fl oz/¾ cup hot water

Marinate the pieces of hare in the wine and vinegar with all the flavourings and spices overnight (or for as long as possible). Drain, reserving the marinade.

In a large frying pan, heat the olive oil and brown the meat. Transfer to a flameproof dish. Brown the shallots in the frying pan and then add to the casserole dish. Add the marinade and tomato paste mixture. Simmer for 2 hours or until the sauce has thickened and the meat and shallots are tender. Alternatively, bake in the oven preheated to 170°C/325°F/Gas Mark 3 for 3 hours.

Right: Lagos Stifado, *hare stew with shallots.*

Mountains, Lakes and Plains

We are back again in autumn.
  Summer,
Like a copybook which has
  wearied us, remains
Full of words crossed out, pen
  strokes scribbled in the margin
And question marks.

– A Word for Summer
by George Seferis

Above: Ikonostassi *(shrines) are found all over Greece.* Left: *The triple peaks of Gamilla, Epirus.*

Mainland Greece sometimes seems like a world forgotten, bypassed on the way to the islands, ignored by the hedonistic sun-seekers in search of a good time at the beach. Another country of mountain forests and streams, wide fertile plains and deserted lakes screened by bullrushes and croaking frogs and always the sudden glimpse of the coaches as they charge around the classical ruins on their three-day tours.

Everyone seems to be on the road for, apart from the fast internal flights to all corners of the country, it is the cheapest and only way of getting around. Long-distance haulage trucks thunder down from a morning start in Tito Veles in Yugoslavia, anxious to off-load their containers in Thessaloniki. A BMW, the status-symbol car in Greece, is on a leisurely weekend cruise to a mountain retreat, speeding past the ever-present local fruit-sellers behind their vans or in makeshift kiosks with bananas, plastic bags of lemons from Arta, apricots from Veria, and apples from Pelion. Anything locally grown is grabbed by those road-running the country.

Because they are so close to the land, Greeks, perhaps more than other nations, like to stop and eat and admire their country when they are travelling around. They will frequently make an impromptu picnic out of local ingredients in some lay-by with a dramatic view of Mount Olympus and its vineyards or beside a spring webbed by a canopy of chestnut trees.

In dusty, grimy market-town squares, the slow diesel trucks stop for doner kebab, *gyros* or loukanika, spicy sausages, served in pitta bread always with a handful of chips, chopped tomato, onion and parsley, a squeeze of ketchup and mustard. A place like Kalambaka survives on the

Left: *Lake Kastoria in Northern Greece.*

Right: *Kamena Vouria, a spa town by the sea, has shops that sell locally made types of pasta like* hilopittes *and* kritharaki.

Following pages: *A flock of sheep graze with the mountains of Northern Greece in the distance.*

coaches passing through to Meteora and its monasteries perched on their granite rocks. The square in this tourist toy-town is a linguist's nightmare with misspelt dishes on the multilingual menus of the restaurants that do a decent *kokkoretsi* and kebab.

On the National Road northwards to Thessaloniki out of Athens, there are established stops for food and drink. In Ekali and Drossia, past the wealthy suburb of Kifissia (with its own clutch of renowned tavernas with gardens that are visited at weekends), are the *penirli* restaurants. These serve boat-shaped open doughs with fillings, cooked in ovens like pizzas. The most common fillings are minced meat or cheese as in Turkey, from where the dish originates as a common street food called *peynerli*.

The next stop is at Kamena Vourla, a spa town before Lamia, where the shops sell locally made *hilopittes* (egg noodles) and *kritharaki* (rice-shaped pasta) from nearby Ipati. The Argo is where everyone eats. Standard restaurant food from the counter like *briam* (a vegetable stew), *moschari me kidonia* (beef with quinces), *domates gemistes* (stuffed tomatoes) and *gigantes*

Above· *Shepherds with their flocks dominate the roads of mountainous Zagorochorio.*

Right: *Loyal goats follow their owner in Halkidiki.*

amastikoto (slightly sweeter), *raki* and *mastika*, all with old-fashioned labels sold among the bottles of local co-operative wines and pottery.

Landscape imposes restrictions that keep the country free of ugly motorways and the mountain regions remain uncompromising places to visit. There are no quick routes into these regions, only the same twisting, dangerous tracks that the mule trains, pack horses and carriages used to slowly take. Journeys can sometimes take just as long, a lazy traipse when stuck behind the modern lorries with supplies bound for remote villages. Landscape also directly affects the cuisine of mainland Greece. The fertile mountains of Epirus, plains of Thrace and lakes of Macedonia, all rich in game and freshwater fish, seem so immediately different from traditional images of the barren Greece of the islands because of one thing – water. This is brought, through automatic sprinklers on the plains or small viaducts in the hills, to smallholdings and orchards in Pelion, vineyards creeping across the hills in Zitsa, the endless fields of *kalamboki* (maize) and tobacco in the flatlands of Thrace.

The roads inland always seem to traverse the largest plains in Greece: Thessaliki, north of Larissa, with its cereals; and Kopaida, close to Thebes, with its cotton, tobacco and almond trees that end up curling beneath the foothills of Mount Parnassus. Here in Roumeli, the true heartland of Greece lurks in the fields and foothills. Women are bent picking the cotton plants that the large mechanical harvesters cannot reach; a shepherd is crouched on a stone watching all the activity with his picnic of bread, cheese and olives, the lazy afternoons in the *kafeneia* discussing the harvest.

The *laiki agora* weekly market is always an event for the local farming families who come into market towns like Amficlea. Once a year, the gypsies come to town for five days and the market becomes even more colourful. Loudspeakers blare monotonous clarinet music from the square where the *souvlaki* stalls sell skewers

plaki (giant beans baked in the oven). There are also favoured pit-stops at garages, where the bus drivers usually receive some commission and a free meal, for the coaches and hapless tourists. Inside, there is always a special dish of the day like *bakaliaros me skordalia* (salt cod and garlic sauce) to keep the truckers happy and row upon row of cheaply made *halvas* and *loukoumi* (Turkish delight) and sweets for the children, all produced in factories around Lamia.

Tirnavos is another stop-over town whose shops do good business with its famous ouzo and wine from the Rapsani vineyards, at the foot of Mount Olympus. The Katsaros company make four types of aniseed drink – ouzo, ouzo

Left: *Dawn mists shroud the mountain villages of Pelion.*

Left: *Dawn mists shroud the mountain villages of Pelion.*

of pork sprinkled with oregano and lemon juice. A normally sedate road in the centre of town is lined with vans and underneath their striped awnings, the trestle tables are laid with tempting goods for the hard-working families. Leather and military jackets on clothes rails, tablecloths and linen dominate the first part of the market.

Then come the cheap cassettes of middle-of-the-road Greek singers like Yiannis Parios and George Dalaras. One man just sells different sized copper bells for sheep and goats; another lays his crude hunting knives out, all the time inscribing the blades with simple proverbs and the date. There is a gypsy hammering out the *briki* (copper coffee makers) to go on copper trays and a widow who has brought down her

Below: *Makrinitsa square with its small chapel and ancient plane tree.*

bags of fragrant herbs from Parnassus to sell. A *kantina* (mobile van) grills sausages sold in sliced rolls and a small boy holds out a clutch of hand-carved olive wood spoons. Everyone goes back to sparsely furnished houses with some new small decoration, maybe a tin tray with flowers on it and more tools for the constant toil with the soil.

Outside Amficlea, the road leads through Lilea to Eptalofos and its tavernas, visited at weekends or used for wedding celebrations. The water taps are fastened to the huge chestnut tree in the square, surrounded with chopped wood for winter use. The orange school bus comes from the town below with half a dozen children who rush home to eat. The taverna in the square, Stamatis, has some of the best mountain-reared lamb, *revithia me domates* (chick-peas stewed with tomatoes), *trachana*, strong *feta* cheese and *brussco*, a petillant new red wine of the region. Typical dishes not often eaten in such peaceful surroundings. From here, the old road leads to Parnassus, past blackberry bushes and a monastery with ice-cold water from a spring, and beyond Arachova, its busy ski resort. Below lies Delphi and the famous vale of ancient olive trees around Amfissia that produce some of the best large fleshy olives in Greece, in mottled grey and brown colours. And then comes the Gulf of Corinth with the Peloponnese across the choppy water.

Mount Pelion, curled like a scorpion's tail with inaccessible fishing village, Trikeri, at its tip, is one of the places Greeks like to holiday. All year round, lured by the good mountain food and scenery. It is, of course, the mythical mountain of centaur legend and mortal heroes Jason and the Argonauts who set off from Iolkos, present-day Volos, beneath its wooded slopes, on the quest for that Golden Fleece.

In winter, Pelion attracts all kinds of people. Honeymooners stay in the cold, grand silk merchant mansions in Vizitsa and Tsangarada where the only way to keep warm is local *tsipouro* (like grappa) and the bed. Art historians

pay homage to the work of Theophilos, the primitive painter 'discovered' in 1928 by some educated patrons who saw him as a Greek Douanier Rousseau. He lived as a travelling craftsman going from village to village and town to town, painting and decorating the walls of tavernas, butchers and bakeries, grocery shops and even windmills for the petty-bourgeois merchants and landowners. Much of the time in Pelion, where his wall-paintings survive in the rich landowner Kontos' house in Anakasia, the bakery in Alo Meria, both in the environs of Ano Volos, and in the *kafeneon* at Makrinitsa. They, alone, are worth the pilgrimage to Pelion as testimony to the way this sad artist lived, dressed always in his *foustanella* (pleated skirt), painting only for his daily food and bread. He asked for nothing more as he worked on his sombre scenes based on incidents from the Greek War of Independence (1821) and contemporary life. It is a vision, steeped also in mythology, and his 'discovery' helped spark the rebirth of Greek popular art with later painters like Tsarouchis, who in his turn painted everyday scenes from Greek life. Theophilos is interesting because he represents the tradition of folk art that adorns shop signs everywhere and the search through art for a form of authentic Greekness.

In Ano Meria, the *fourno* oven, once owned by Velenzas, an immigrant from the Black Sea, has nine impressive murals. Two are very famous – a circus strong-man wrestling a lion which was a favourite subject and, the lovers Erotokritos and Aretousa, taken from the seventeenth-century Cretan masterpiece 'Erotokritos' by Kornaros. This is the long and subversive poem that kept the spirit of Hellenism alive during the Cold War years of the Venetian occupation, now part of the national heritage.

Pelion is also skiing country, around Xania, where there are 150-year-old mountain inns called *hani*. Only one still preserves any architectural beauty. The Manthos *hani*, down a steep road, look up towards the slopes. A stove keeps the guests warm and toasts bread on its hot metal top, a favourite winter pursuit. This is a place that serves the real earthy specialities of the region. *Spetsofai*, one of the most representative dishes of Greece, is a simple mix of coarse country sausages and green peppers. *Fasolia gigantes*, large beans baked in the oven or made into soup, *gida vrasti*, boiled goat that has something of the fragrance of a simple *bollito misto*. *Galotiri*, piquant lumps of soft goats cheese with paprika, stews like *hirino me prassa* (pork and leeks) or *me selino* (with celery) and *kotopoulo kokkinisto* ('reddened' chicken) all reflect the need for warming food in a harsh mountain climate.

In Pelion, the *omihli* (mist) descends blindingly, halting cars on the winding roads. The men are forced into the tavernas and cafés, misted up by this thick fog or the snow. Clogged in solitude and the soporific haze of *tsipouro*, motionless by the stoves, watching the Brazilian soap-operas at 5pm for darkness falls stealthily in Pelion, cloaking the mountain villages in anonymity, only the smell of smoke from innumerable wood fires reveals their existence.

Visitza and Milies are two villages that reveal their secrets more easily. Both being actively restored to their former glory after the earthquake of 1955, they have large eighteenth-century mansions, built with the wealth from olives and mulberry trees (the raw silk was exported to Chios weavers). A great frost in 1782 destroyed many olive trees but they were replanted with cherry trees from the Peloponnese, giving the landscape a much softer feel in spring.

Milies is the grander of the two with an impressive library from its days as a centre of learning in the nineteenth century and a small museum dedicated to artisan skills still practised like wood and stone carving. Local life used to centre around the railway station which opened the village up to the outside world but was closed in 1971. The small train from Volos brought day-trippers and merchandise across

The village home is always well-kept and brightly painted.

the bridges (built by Italian engineers headed by the surrealist painter Giorgio di Chirico's father) and into the hills. Milies became, in effect, one of the first resorts in Pelion for the local townsfolk of Volos. The line is due to re-open again soon and the train nicknamed 'Moundzouris' ('old smokey') will take the people of Volos, where there is a thriving 'light' food and drink industry back to the Aigli *kafeneon* shaded by ancient plane trees in the square.

Visitza, the smaller village, manages to disappear into the hillside. The mansions have been turned into guest houses by EOT, the Greek tourist board, but despite the tourists, the place seems to ignore its role as 'model village'. The mansions have, perhaps, been too immaculately restored with central heating and it is only the wood smoke from the fires of the real, dilapidated houses beyond the square, that reveal where the true village is. A cobbled path leads into the deep chestnut woods, past springs and smouldering fires of collected leaves, where an old man is picking wild mushrooms. In Greece, *manitaria* (mushrooms) are regarded with suspicion and there are often reports of poisoning. People are not as obsessed as the Spaniards or Italians with the mushroom forage. There are no illustrated handbooks but most villagers will pick half a dozen recognized, safe varieties like horse, field and parasol mushrooms, chanterelle and oyster mushrooms, and there is certainly mention of the truffle in ancient Greek texts, if little evidence of the obsessive and highly commercial search for it undertaken by other countries.

Visitza's square is quiet in winter. The fountain trickles water and the tables and chairs are stacked until better weather arrives. Only the lights from the general store and the *kafeneon* called 'Georgaras', glow into the dark night. Inside, the men of the village are eating *poupai* (a local blood sausage) with rice and drinking the fruity *moscato*, the red wine of the region. A group of Polish men, working on the restoration of one of the mansions, are listening to the conversations, trying to learn the language, happy with the heavy, warming food of winter.

There is a bakery beneath the two villages that people drive from miles around to visit. A modern efficient oven produces *eliopsomo*, *tiropsomo* and one of the best, commercially baked, pies in the area, a *hortopitta* made with seven types of local *horta* and herbs. There are also jars of homemade *kidonia* (quince) and *phirikia* (apple stuffed with almonds) and *karydia* liqueur, made from steeping walnuts in their green shells with sugar and later adding brandy.

Tsangarada and Zagora show Pelion at its most productive. This is apple country, and the orchards cling to the hillsides in a haze of red that almost reaches the sea below. *Phirikia* are the famed, small crisp apples of the region, piled up in wooden boxes in mid-November, waiting to be collected and taken to the local co-operative. Some farmers sell them by the road, along with *aktinidia* (kiwi fruit) and large marrows.

This is the coastal Pelion of steep cliffs and sandy beaches to rival those of the island of Skiathos opposite. The villagers do not have to eat *bakaliaros* or *renga* (herring) for they have access to the fresh fish caught by the caiques of Horefto. These are launched from the long beach in winter, the fishermen gather in the one restaurant that remains open with its log fire blazing when they come back, leaving their waterproofs and boots outside. Two sisters run the 'Gorgones' restaurant, getting up from their seats by the fire, to prepare the food. *Galeos* (dogfish or huss) is a favourite dish fried in batter and served with strong *skordalia* (garlic dip) and cabbage salad. Down here, the *omihli* (mist) cannot be seen but the waves come crashing in off the miserable grey sea.

In northern Greece, the Balkan influence is as strong as the smell of Turkish cigarettes smoked constantly in the cafés. In the border towns and villages of Macedonia and Thrace, cultures clash and deserted villages are the price paid by war. In eastern Thrace, the Rodopi mountains border

Autumn brings wild mushrooms to the woods and fields, picked with care by cautious villagers.

The bakery near Milies, in the heart of Pelion, makes delicious eliopsomo *(olive bread) and* tiropsomo *(cheese bread).*

Bulgaria and surround Pomaki villages like Smigada and Organi with military camps. The Pomaki are a Slavic muslim minority with their own language and customs. Visitors are not encouraged (it needs special permission) in this sensitive border area but they often come down to Komotini and its weekly Tuesday market. The women in their *yashmaks* and men in baggy trousers, wander the old Turkish quarter with its small bazaar of tinsmiths that leads to a modern enclosed market selling spicy *loukanika* sausages and smoked fish. The smell of roasting chick-peas and ground coffee is everywhere in this modern town where half the population is muslim. The Greeks like to congregate in places like the Xenia Hotel, its restaurant packed on a Saturday night with people eating *soutzoukakia* (meatballs in the Smyrna style) and *horta*.

Beyond Komotini, the real Thrace of the plains begins; the villages are divided. A minaret and church spire wink at each other across fields in the reflecting sun. Aratos has men squatting outside their improverished Anatolian houses; Arsakio and Sapes are typical Greek villages with well-kept squares and churches. Nearing the coast and the scenery of olive groves and almond orchards, the familiar Greece of the Aegean sea, returns. It is as if all the clichés were true, that Greece really is about the smell and colour of that 'wine-dark' sea. And nearby Alexandroupolis is a very Greek town. The stopping point for Greek holiday-makers returning from nostalgic trips to the city. 'Polis' (or Constantinople as the Greeks like to call Istanbul) who immediately rush into the tavernas and *kafeneia* for a taste of the homeland again; fried fish, pork *souvlakia* and *pastitsio* (baked pasta and meat pie).

There are ferries from here to isolated Samothrace, also a very Greek island, remote and untouched by historical changes. It is a mysterious place dominated by the highest mountain in the Aegean, Mount Fengari, snow-capped for much of the year, with slopes that hide therapeutic hot springs and waterfalls. There are tavernas in the hills near streams, that serve *tirino-pittes* (cheese pies) made with *mezithra* cheese, rice and fresh mint or a *stifado* made with wild rabbit or hare. The fish are plentiful too in this island that catches the annual migration of fish from the Black Sea. Its desolation hides one of the best sited ancient ruins in Greece, the temple of the Great Gods, with its view of Mount Fengari, at Paleopolis, where the pre-Hellenic cult of the Great Gods and the Eleusian Mysteries became a pilgrimage of the ancient world. The statue of the Winged Victory (Nike), now in the Louvre, was also found here.

Close to Turkey, the Evros Wetlands are home to wild duck and many other migratory birds like flamingos. The border towns, Didimotichon, Soufli and Orestiada, are defiantly Greek but across the border everything changes. It is another world, another culture kept at bay by the River Evros. Soufli, with its mulberry trees is known for its raw silk; Didimotichon is a small Byzantine town with history and a very old mosque to prove it, and Orestiada – the last modern town before Kastanies and the crossing over to present-day Edirne, still known as Adrianopolis in Greece.

Crossing over to Edirne, 8 miles (12.5 km) away, the modern differences between Greek and Turkish cuisine become apparent. The small *lokantsi* restaurant near the towering sixteenth-century Selimiye Mosque, serves *kofte* (meat-balls), *pilav* (rice) and a watery *fasulye* stew (as opposed to the rich oven-baked *fasolia* of Greece). There are small cups of tea instead of wine and something of the East in the hushed atmosphere while eating. In Greece, there would have been a lot more noise, for even the humblest meal is turned into a celebration.

The road back to Greece, passes a restaurant with handwritten sign saying 'Zesto kreas sto piato' (literally 'hot meat on the plate'). This is the only indication to motorists that it is the road back home. An irony not lost on those who like to put their money where their mouths are. For, where East meets West, it is a cold and hot war waged through the stomach, a final bid to extract foreign currency from the Greeks.

But even in the border towns, what food that is available in tavernas shows its influences in Turkish dishes like *tsiro-psarmas*, a 'rolled' dish of minced liver, cheese and bechamel, fried like a *borek* (Turkish pastry) in this region, but baked in other parts of Greece. It is easy to see how a cuisine both divides and unites different nations.

Thrace remains inaccessible, its best cuisine hidden behind the closed doors of the family home. It is only in big towns like Xanthi that the apartheid stops. There is always a Saturday open air market in Xanthi and during Apokries, the pre-Lenten Carnival in February, the streets really come alive. This is when families, both Muslim and Greek, Pomaki and gypsy, come into town. If the weather is good, the old-fashioned fairground attractions and stalls do good business. The children go to fancy dress parties while their parents go their separate ways. The men head for the *zachoroplasteon* (cake shop) in the Old Town for *ravani* (a rich semolina sponge) and *rizogalo* (rice pudding), coffee and cigarettes. The women are trying the cheap colognes or buying material from the gypsy stalls. The food is on the streets as well, standard *souvlaki* or sausages, grilled enthusiastically by

the salesmen as they take the grubby 100 drachmae bills from young children dressed in cardboard hats and carrying cardboard swords.

In Kavala, there is the best fish restaurant in northern Greece. Not surprisingly, it is next to the harbour and the deep-water fishing boats that off-load their catches into the market every day. The people of Kavala are lucky to live in a city that is the country's most elegant port. Shadowed by the remains of a sixteenth-century aquaduct and well-preserved Turkish buildings like Mehmet Ali's house and harem, is Zafeira, and two other restaurants that live off its reputation.

At Zafeira, the menu is long and the waiters obviously bored with reciting the daily specials. It is best to go into the kitchen and examine the pots. Apart from the freshly grilled fish, sold by weight, there are some classic dishes here. *Midia saganaki* (mussels baked with tomatoes and herbs), *soupies yiachni* (cuttlefish stewed with onions), *gavros sto fourno* (baked anchovies) and one of their specialities, *bakaliaros me skordalia* (salt cod and garlic sauce). The local wine is Mayrommatis *retsina*, the place for coffee is the *kafeneon* almost next door where the old merchant houses, now shipping agents, line the harbour.

If Kavala shows its Turkish history in some of the food available in the tavernas, like *manti* (the pasta 'ravioli' filled with meat and served with yoghurt), then Thessaloniki – or Salonika – positively revels in its cosmopolitan origins. Not only the Turks but more importantly historically the largest Jewish community in Greece thrived in this city. There were 70,000 of them with thirty-two synagogues, and Ladino as their language, and they gave the city a predominantly Jewish and Spanish air until the great fire of 1917 destroyed the Jewish quarter of the city and many were forced to emigrate. The German occupation of Greece in 1941 and the subsequent deportation to the Polish death camps, destroyed the community's influence but many recipes survive. One greengrocer, who speaks

Ladino, still has a shop, for the few remaining Jews in the city. Dishes like *sazan con babottes* (carp with greengage sauce), *poyo con prounes* (chicken with prunes), *pastel de kweso* (cheese pie with sesame seeds), *fritadas* ('tortillas') and *ayran* (the yoghurt and water drink) are all Jewish recipes from the city, that show their Spanish, Turkish and Greek origins both in their ingredients and names.

Thessaloniki is renowned for its good restaurants and there is one that typifies the metropolitan feel of the city. Krikelas, on the road east to the Souroti springs (where one of the best mineral waters is bottled), is a huge basement *estiatorion*, which, in true democratic Greek style, everyone knows about. There are black and white photographs of blonde sixties' starlets on the walls and waiters who have served there for years. The menu is long and proudly reveals its Turkish influences among the Macedonian dishes. For the many businessmen who visit , there are also expense-account items like smoked salmon, caviar, canned Russian crabs, *Bitok à la Russe* and *schnitzel*.

The *orektika* (hors d'oeuvres) have an interesting selection of smoked, salted and dried meat and fish dishes. *Likourini* (smoked grey mullet), *tsirosalata* (dried mackerel), *avgotaracho*, smoked eel and trout and *pastourma*. Real *pastourma* came from Turkey where it is traditionally made from lean camel meat. Exiles from Smyrna and other areas of Aegean Turkey (who left in the 1922 exchange of populations) search nostalgically for it in Istanbul markets. Greek *pastourma* is made from ox-meat, salted with spices and dried or smoked, it can be found in most Greek shops.

It is with the meat dishes that the Macedonian influence becomes apparent. Game like *agriopapia* (wild duck), *bekatsa* (woodcock), ortikia (quail), *fassianos* (pheasant), *tsikles* (thrushes), *agrioperistera* (wild pigeon), *agriohiro* (wild pig), and *mezedakia ortikion* (quail entrails in sauce) are available in the hunting season.

Near Albania, an old shepherd with a large flock sells all his milk to a nearby co-operative.

Far right: Ruined mud-brick houses characterize deserted villages like Gavros on the way to the Prespa lakes.

There are also Turkish dishes like *Gialantzi dolmas* (stuffed vine leaves), *tsoblek kebab* (a beef and vegetable kebab) and *doudourmas salep* (ice-cream made from *salep*, an orchid root).

The road to the Prespa Lakes from Kastoria, like all the border roads in isolated parts of Greece, is eerily quiet. Signs say 'No hunting allowed' in case the gun shots are misunderstood in nearby Albania, where many ethnic Greeks live, a number of them exiles from the Civil War years. Kristallopigi is the last village before the Albanian border crossing; a solitary taxi taking a passenger back to that mysterious, backward country, hoots at the shepherd and his large flock of sheep blocking his path. The only buildings looked after in these deserted villages are the churches. At Gavros, the earth and wattle houses are in ruins, an abandoned school littered with old text-books and papers, overgrown with wild mint. The red earth bricks still keep the house warm for the last elderly couple who live there. At Vrondero, the old shepherd with 400 sheep is herding them into thatched pens. He sells all the milk to a nearby factory that makes *feta* cheese.

Greeks make the pilgrimage to the remote lakes for three reasons – the freshwater fish at

Above left: *At Psarades, on the shores of Megali Prespa, the tavernas serve freshly caught carp and trout, pepper and beetroot salads with carafes of red wine.*

Above right: Tsironia, *salty, sun-dried freshwater fish when barbecued are a perfect accompaniment to* ouzo.

Far right: *One of the flat-bottomed punts used to catch huge carp at Mikra Prespa.*

the humble tavernas, the bird-watching and the border setting. Megali (Big) Prespa is the highest lake in the Balkans and from Psarades, day-trippers take a xenophobic trip by speed-boat to the point where the Yugoslav, Albanian and Greek borders meet. On a day when the tour-buses from Thessaloniki are absent, the village of Psarades goes back into its lazy cocoon of inactivity. Cocks are fighting in the street and a fisherman is tarring the bottom of his punt. The tavernas are empty and ready for business. At the 'Parodosi Psarotaverna' (fish taverna) the tables block the street. The only thing to eat are the fresh *petalouda* (roach), *platikes* (carp) and *pestrofa* (trout). These are fried with flour and served with plates of *patsaria* (garlicky beet-root), *piperies* (pickled red peppers), the strong local *feta* and jugs of local red wine made near Florina.

In the wooden balconied houses by the lake, their courtyards stacked with fire-wood and hanging strings of red peppers, there is one man who sells *tsironia*, small freshwater fish that are salted and dried in the sun. These are for cooking on charcoal and then eating when drinking ouzo.

Mikri (small) Prespa is an ornithologist's paradise. The nesting ground for the Dalmation pelican, little bittern, cormorants, eagles and egrets. At Mikrolimni, there is one restaurant-shop with rooms to let. This is less of a tourist stop and more of a working village. The fisher-men leave in their long punts to lay their nets early in the morning and collect them in the evening except for the time between 15 April and 10 June when the fish are spawning. The huge scaly primeval-looking carp overload the punts on the journey back through the reeds to the rickety wooden jetty. Here, there is a rusting weighing machine for the fish which are then boxed for transportation to the markets of northern Greece. It is only in recent years that

the Greeks have begun to eat freshwater fish. They have always been considered unclean, the fish of poverty but now smoked trout especially, appears on many of the menus in the new Athenian restaurants.

The fields around the lakes both here and in Kastoria, are perfect for growing *fasolia* (haricot beans), on wooden wigwam frames. Farmers sell kilo bags of the highly prized beans, one of the Greeks' favourite foods, from roadside stalls.

Florina, 18 miles (29 km) from Yugoslavia, is the place for peppers. If nearby Yugoslavia has any influence, it is in these red peppers, that appear in shops and in restaurants, universally known as *piperies Florinis*. In the local market, they dominate the stalls, along with wrinkled dried and thin *kafteres*, light green peppers, used in Greece for the dish *piperies tiganites* (fried in olive oil). There is a shop that sells nothing but jars of the pickled crimson peppers and *pipero-saltsa glykia* (sweet red pepper sauce).

The early morning mist shrouds the fishermen of Kastoria, in winter one of the coldest places to be in Greece. It is also one of the

Collecting windfallen oranges.

wealthiest. The 'nouveau riche' of Kastoria drive in BMWs and Mercedes; a long mainstreet is lined with shops that sell the 'designer label' clothes beloved by the young. Much of the money comes from the established fur industry which imports scraps from America, Canada and Russia and turns them into coats; nobody seems to care about animal rights here. The rest comes from emigrants from America, who have made it good and return to restore the family homes. They like to spend their money in style, in the pizza restaurants and expensive bars like the Coco Pub by the lake. It lives up to its winter nickname of the 'St Moritz of Greece'.

But 'old' Kastoria is a place of surprising beauty; there are over seventy churches, many with fine Byzantine frescos, and some well-preserved eighteenth-century *archontika*, the three-storey wooden panelled houses of the old fur-merchants. One, the mansion of the Aivazis family is now the folk museum and recreates the grand, self-sufficient lifestyle of the past.

There is a market every Tuesday and Saturday on different shores of this town built on a promontory that juts out into the lake. The lake

The kafeneon *by the lake-side fish market in Kastoria.*

shore road, past Mavrotissa monastery, is where the rod fishermen congregate for hours on end. If the snow-capped mountains, plane trees and swans were not there, it could be any island scene in the Aegean.

The enclosed market spills out to the lake on Tuesdays and the stall-holders come in from surrounding villages with produce. In winter, there are red and green peppers, stumps of *selinorizzo* (celeriac), cabbage and beetroot, bunches of dill and spring onions, oranges and apples. Some of the traders speak in the guttural border tongue of the region as they trim bright cauliflowers of their outer leaves. By the lake itself, the fishermen sell shiny silver roach and writhing carp directly from their punts, weighing them in the scales and into the plastic carrier bags of rosy-cheeked widows who have walked down the steep hill. This is a market worth the steep walk down from the town and in May, when the strawberries of the region are brought in from the hills, it is busier than usual.

The faded *kafeneon* by the shore, has escaped the ugly modernization that is happening elsewhere. The owner Dimitri caters for the fishermen and their simple tastes on cold mornings. Ouzo is served with *mezedes* of strong pickled cabbage and carrot. There is a stove in the middle of the room that keeps warm an old-fashioned *gioumi* (water container). The past is important here and the walls are lined with photographs and behind the counter, two hookahs (water-pipes) lie idle.

There is only one really old fashioned taverna in the town, near the curch of Agios Nikolaos, that is crowded every night. No fish is cooked in this taverna in the old town, only rich meat dishes like *soutzoukakia*, *biftekia me tiri* (beef wrapped around local salty cheese and peppers), *gida vrasti* and a fiery *tirosalata* (soft cheese and pepper dip), the type of food not often made at home by the wives of the hard drinking men who sit in dark workrooms all day sewing together the pelts of locally-farmed minks with scraps from the New World.

Left: *One of the Turkish-built bridges of the Zagorochorio.*

In isolated Epirus to the south, hemmed in by the Pindus Mountains like Smolikas and Gamila, poverty through war led to mass emigration which deadened many parts of Greece, but the area has always been fed by mountain streams and rivers with trout and crayfish, and forests where game like wild boar and venison roam. Survival, for those versed in the lore of this land, has never been difficult. Nomad Vlach and Sarakatsani wandered with their flocks, and villages in the Zagoria enjoyed autonomy and prosperity under the Turks by paying an annual tribute.

Metsovo, the Vlach capital, became a wealthy trading point, the surrounding villages traded mountain produce like cheese and woollen goods; and Ioannina, the capital of Epirus, became a centre of great learning. Nothing has changed. Metsovo is more commercially minded than ever, the mountain villages are traditionally restored for the expanding new trade in eco-tourists who come to hike and Ioannina is a thriving university town.

Perhaps the new prosperity makes people seem friendlier than the normally reticent people of most mountain areas. Shepherds shout greetings over the incessant clanging of sheep-bells, a woman offers wild flowers she has just

Right: *Kyria Eleni in her courtyard in Mazion.*

Above: *Kyria Eleni rolls home-made* filo *pastry and pours olive oil between layers of the* tiropitta *(cheese-pie) that she is making.*

Left: *Many Greeks make their own* vissinada *(cherry jam) in the autumn.*

picked, a child leads hikers up to the mountain stream.

In Mazion, smiling Kyria Eleni gives a warm welcome from her open door. If the kitchen is the centre of life in Aegean islands, it is the courtyard that is more important in the Epirot village house. In spring, the cherry tree that grows inside the courtyard, is picked and she makes *vissino glyko* (cherry jam) outside, pitting the cherries into a large *tapsi*. Now that it is sunny, she does all her cooking outside in the oven built into the wall.

In Epirus, *pittes* made with meat, chicken, *horta*, cheese and fruit are the speciality. *Hiti* (a coarse bread) and *roussanitses* (similar to *trachana*) known by its Slavic name, *pligouri* (cracked wheat) are popular; and mountain-reared lamb or goat, cheese and seasonal vegetables form the main diet.

In winter, the courtyard is stacked with wood, and after the wine has been made in November, the *tsipouro* is distilled, like Grappa, from the grape skins and stalks. Each family borrows the local primitive pot still from the church, lights a fire underneath it and then waits for the slow distillation of the first drops of lethal liquid. The neighbours arrive for an impromptu party also awaiting the first drops of new *tsipouro*.

In summer, the courtyard trellis is covered in vines and there are pots of basil, parsley and purslane. Kyria Eleni makes a *tiropitta* (cheese pie) in the shade. She sets her *tavla*, the low round table used for making pastry, out and mixes a simple *zymari* (dough) out of flour and water. The filling is made with beaten eggs, *feta* and *mezithra* cheeses, crumbled and grated. She then rolls the dough into thin layers of pastry with a special long rolling pin, called a *matsoxilo*

Left: Mikro Papingo huddles beneath the peaks of Gamila.

or *plasti*. Two of these are layered over the edge of a *tapsi*, the mixture put in, and another two layers on top and then folded over. Years of almost daily practice have made her very quick with pies, the equivalent of fast food for the family.

Mazion is in an enviable position between the towering Mount Gamila and the Konitsa plain of wheat fields below, irrigated by the River Aoos that flows through a small valley providing ideal pasture for the livestock of the village. Behind, lies Aetopetra, Melissopetra and finally Molythoskepasto (or Molitho) on the border with Albania, with its thirteenth-century Byzantine church of the Holy Apostles. This is flood-lit at night for Albanian Greeks to see.

At Aetopetra, one enterprising Albanian Greek who fled a few years ago has restored an old hunting lodge and farms game, mostly venison and boar, nearby. His Bourazani Hotel is packed at weekends with people who came to try unusual venison *moussaka*, *kapros* (boar) and fresh trout from the river outside. The place, with its stuffed deer and antelope and expensive prices, in such an inaccessible area, is regarded with suspicion by the villagers of Mazion.

Theocharis sits at the cramped table, cluttered with old society magazines and week-old newspapers, some brittle tooth-picks in a maroon melamine container and a jug of new olive-green wine. He takes glasses and a brand new telephone out of the wall cupboard, his face crumpling into a smile as he fumbles with the receiver, trying to dial his wife in the lower village of Megalo Papingo. 'We have guests who are hungry and want a room for the night', he tells her.

The two villages of Papingo are the last settlements before the imposing Pyrgi, the three towers at the head of the Vikos Gorge and Gamila beyond. Mikro Papingo is the most beautiful village in the western Zagoria, its houses carved defiantly out of the local slate and stone, the narrow cobbled streets tapering off into the steep paths past covered springs like the

Vrissi Abragonios on the long route up to the mountain peaks with their lakes, rare wild flowers and stunning views towards Albania.

Megalo Papingo is the more worldly of the two villages. Tourism takes over from shepherding as the traditional pursuit. The tavernas are used to ravenous hikers and serve fresh trout from the River Voidomatis below, tender pink roast mountain goat from the slopes and baked *kidonia* (quince) or cherries depending on the season.

Between the two villages, a stream runs through a narrow gorge of waterfalls and eddies filled with orange-bellied toads and salamanders bathing in the sun. In the evening, the goats are led through the streets of Mikro Papingo by the shepherdess into dark medieval pens laid with straw.

Only twenty people live permanently in the village, many of them old like Theocharis and his wife Elizabetta who looks after the EOT rooms in the restored houses. Meals are taken in their cramped small kitchen with its slow-cooking oven that provides heat in the centre of the room. The food of Zagoria, as in all the other mountain regions of the country, is based on the occasionally slaughtered meat and the fresh

Right: Mountain shepherds always travel with their sturdy aglitses (crooks) and colourful bags often filled with some cheese and bread for the lonely hours guarding their flocks.

vegetables that grow in small cultivated gardens. If that is a monotonous diet for many people, for the 46 villages of Zagoria, it is a diet that binds them to their sometimes inhospitable land. As Elizabetta takes the *tapsi* out of the oven the smell of the roast is an unconscious celebration, the survival through their flocks, of these mountain people. Theocharis silently pours the wine as the wind howls outside the window. A window that looks out on the lights of the village below and the black peaks above. An owl hoots in the starless night, the eagle is asleep in his mountain lair and the twenty inhabitants of the village are all eating quietly, their lives governed totally by the seasons.

Metsovo, whichever way it is approached, either from Ioannina over the high Katara Pass or from Meteora and its monasteries, is always busy. The roads bring the skiers in the winter, the tourist buses in the summer. They all come to see this town of contradictions where the people work hard and worship money. The Vlachs, noble and proud they may be, but their determination to survive causes moral dilemmas somewhere. Where once they roamed with their flocks across the Balkans, they now drive their new pick-up trucks to permanent pastures in the lowlands around Ioannina. The traditional skills

of wood-carving, embroidery and textiles are in every shop and every public place. Old men and women, in particular, dress in their own costumes, the women with embroidered shawls and long skirts, and gather around the famous bus-stop in the square where the cameras click in the summer months and the row of cheese shops do an astounding amount of business. Their dialect is a lilting romance language like Romanian that seems to give them the advantage in numerous private discussions in the shops, but has a mesmerizing effect on the listener.

It is like a Disneyland recreation of a model mountain community where the price of entrance is some useless artisan goods like miniature varnished wine barrels and combs. In the process of promoting their own unique heritage, and stressing their contribution to Greece as a country, the Vlachs of Metsovo sacrifice themselves to commerce and all its inherent corruptions. It is a town of immense wealth. Old money displayed in the Tositsa Museum and in the Averoff modern art gallery (not something that many provincial Greek towns can boast) and new money on show in more ostentacious ways, the red tile roofs, huge TV aerials and smart cars. Yet it is a place to marvel at for its industry and the enigma of

Right and bottom right: *The Krinos* zacharoplasteion *(cake shop) in* Ioannina *sells home-made* glyka tou koutaliou *(sweet preserves) and local specialities like* baklavas.

coming to terms with culture in rural Greece.

The food and wine is particularly good; well-organized production and sales of the famed local cheeses made at the *tyrokomeion* (cheese factory) or a red wine called *Katogi*, using grapes from grafted vines from Bordeaux under the auspices of the Averoff family. This is expensive for Greek wine but well worth trying. The cheese co-operative opened thirty years ago and employs fifteen people in the busy production of *metsovone kapnisto* (smoked cow's milk cheese), *graviera*, *parmezana* (parmesan), *sevre me piperi* (chevre with pepper) and a very rich *voutiro* (butter). The cheese unique to Metsovo is *kapnisto*, smoked with vine and plane shavings, then salted for four days, scrubbed in hot water and left to hang before preserving this sausage-shaped cheese in yellow wax. Buying the cheeses from the cheese factory saves 15 per cent on the shop prices and they are glad to show people around.

But, buying from Costas Tseligkas in the town's square is more of an experience. A true salesman, he dresses in the traditional baggy trousers, hat and waistcoat of the Vlach. His moustache hides a wicked grin. His tiny shop, covered in photographs also sells other cheeses

like *manouri* (the sweetish soft sheep's milk cheese), *kasseri* (like Italian provolone) and *mizithra*. It is hard to believe his wealth on visiting his flocks at Perama near Ioannina, where he is building himself a palatial mansion with rooms to let.

The restaurant, To Spitiko, in the main street, is one of the best in the town. Forgetting the mock-rustic surroundings of red check tablecloths and hanging gourds, the food is cooked by a chef who has worked his way around the world on cruise ships, and the Athens Hilton before returning home to add a less chaotic touch than usual. *Trachanosoupa* (Trachana soup), *gida vrasti* and *mayeritsa* are always on the menu. Typical food of the area also available are *lachanopitta*, a filling vegetable pie made with a mixture of burdock, leeks, spinach, spring onions (scallions) and fresh herbs and *keftedes me prassa* (meatballs baked with leeks). Whatever happens in Metsovo, the food and drink will always be worth the journey.

In Ioannina, a thoroughly modern town despite its Ottoman history, the old Turkish quarter and citadel is the area where life has not changed. Women take their daily *tapsia* of stuffed vegetables to the bakery and in a dark

Left: *Retinning copper pots in the old Turkish quarter of Ioannina.*

The daily market in Ioannina where mountain women come down to sell wild horta *and vegetables.*

workroom a man carries on the old tradition of relining copper cooking pots, fanning the charcoal fire with his bellows. The Krinos *zacharoplasteion* (cake shop) makes all its own cakes and sweets that tempt from the clever window display, jars of *glyka* (sweet preserves), *vanilla* and packets of *baklavas Ioanninaion*, a tight cake of honeyed *baklavas*. Another speciality of the town is its *bougatsa*, thin slices, piping hot with cinnamon dusted on top.

In the spring, the daily open air market is one of the best in the country for *horta*. Cheerful Epirot women come in from their mountain and lake-side villages, with sacks and wicker baskets of *spanaki* (spinach), *vlita* (wild beets or goosefoot), *kardamon* (watercress) and *radikia* (dandelion). By the gates of the market, they set up for the long hours of persuasion. A contest begins between two women selling bunches of herbs, trying to outshout each other, in a bid to attract people spoilt for choice. The fresh herbs, dill, parsley, mint and spearmint, are beautifully packaged and tied into bundles, the roots wrapped in vine-leaves like *dolmades* and frequently sprinkled with water to keep them moist. Another woman has baskets of eggs and garlic and bags of bulbs. These are the *agriokremmydia* (wild onions) or *sklyrokremmydia*

A short boat ride takes people to the island on Lake Pamvotis and its tavernas specializing in trout, crayfish and frogs legs.

(hard onions), which are very popular during the Lenten fasting. They were also a favourite food in ancient Greece; the best are supposed to come from Megara in the Peloponnese. *Volvi* are boiled twice to remove traces of bitterness and then eaten as a salad or used in *toursi* (pickled vegetables).

Each stall-holder has something special to tempt the difficult customers. Some *tsouknides* (nettles) that are boiled and given to those with upset stomachs; *roka* (rocket) or Vlach herb and mixes of *horta* (wild greens) called *moschucité* for using in pies. A man with a wheelbarrow of giant and baby leeks and spring onions, blocks the road, anxious to sell as quickly as possible. There are live carp and trout on their sides in baking trays of water, gulping at the surface, the fishermen stroking them affectionately. At lunchtime, the mountain women bring out their frugal picnics of *alethropitta* (flour and cheese pie) and *galatopitta* (sweet egg and milk pies), laughing at the man on the red bicycle wobbling along the road with his leeks tied on the back.

In Ioannina, they practise the very Greek habit of going to specialist restaurants for either meat or fish. Situated on the shores of Lake Pamvotis, the place for seafood is the island of

Nisi Ioannina, 30 minutes away by ferry. The frequent ferries dock outside the restaurants with their tanks, fed by constant pipes of flowing water, and signs promising 'Specialite: Crayfish, Trout, Frogs Legs, mousaka'. Schoolchildren pack the ferries and rush to see the history, the last stand of the tyrant Ali Pasha, murdered on the island. There are sixty fishermen still living with their families in the village of winding streets, where most houses are converted into shops hoping to catch the tourist trade with some tacky trinkets. But the best catches are at the restaurants with tables at the waters edge, all touting for business.

In the tanks, elderly carp that look more like prehistoric coelacanths, perform tricks for a piece of bread, coming by name to the surface, it seems, to eat out of the waiters' hands. The things to eat are the *vatrakia* (frogs legs) or *heli* (eel). Recent pollution, now being cleared up, has affected the fishing, most noticeable in the lack of freshwater crabs. But carp, trout and crayfish are plentiful and there are frogs, caught on a daily basis, everywhere in large buckets. Many are exported to France and provide a modest livelihood for the fishermen. Costas, one

Right: Frogs are the livelihood for about sixty fishermen on the island.

Left: Fishing for atherina *(smelt) with stretched nets dipped into the shallow water of the lagoons around Aetolikon.*

of them, is enthusiastic about their taste when cooked at home. 'The way we cook them, *kokkinisto* with tomato and onions, they taste like *ortikia* (quail).' He is right. In the Gripos restaurant on the front, *pané*, or simply fried in breadcrumbs with lemon juice, they are delicious.

For meat, there is one outstanding restaurant on the road out to the airport, called Gastra. Two owners, Vangelis and Dimitri, never take holidays and oversee the gentle art of *gastra* cooking. This is the method of charcoal baking goat or lamb in Epirus. A large *gastra*, or metal lid, is placed over a *tapsi* of meat, potatoes with oil, lemon juice and sprinkled oregano that is laid on hot tiles warmed by charcoal which is also heaped over the top. This creates a hermetically sealed oven that slow-cooks the meat for two hours. The result is an incredibly tender and moist roast cooked in three 'ovens' three times a day to satisfy the demand. The restaurant also serves another speciality, *stamna* or *stamnaki*, the individual stews cooked in earthenware lidded pots which the waiter brings to the table, removing the lid and upturning the beef or lamb stew cooked with wine, potatoes, tomatoes and carrots. This is undoubtedly one of the best restaurants in northern Greece. Other dishes include *yiaprakia* (*dolmades* stuffed with meat), *lachanodolmades* (cabbage stuffed with rice and *avgolemono* sauce) and *skordalia me karidia* (garlic sauce made with walnuts). The local petillant white from Zitsa made from the *debina* grape is the wine everyone drinks.

At night, Ioannina comes to life in a splutter of neon lights advertising the twilight zone of bars, discotheques and greasy fast-food stops, frequented by the students. One such place, with its faded 1970s' decor is the Arena Club, where local big-spenders like to hold court at tables with red candles under glass, roses in wine bottles and baskets of popcorn. The subdued lighting and early 1980s' soul music is a sad indication of all that is wrong with provincial life of the young. It is not at all fashionable in

the way out west of Greece.

As Epirus moves into Roumeli, the richness of the land is seen again; Arta's citrus groves, Agrinio's dam and irrigation schemes that water the tobacco fields, and greenhouses that grow strawberries and bananas, Messolonghion and Aetolikon's extensive fishing of their surrounding lagoons. Aitoliko, or 'Little Venice' as it is called, is a curious island reached by bridge, where the seventeen fishermen catch *atherina* (smelt) with stretched nets rigged to the masts of flat-bottomed boats that they dip into the shallow waters of the lagoon. Between Aetolikon and Messalonghion, the coastal road passes the salt flats and shambolic gypsy camps. It is impossible not to stop and look, impossible not to be relieved of belongings if naïve. Dark-skinned, black-eyed children mesmerize with their beauty, encircling the innocent as they pick-pocket coins, the price of an ice-cream in nearby Aetolikon. Beneath the tents, gypsy women are frying potatoes on portable gas burners, the men sit smoking and drinking coffee. The elders of the makeshift village warn of the dangers of visiting the tent that stands alone, almost goading the gullible onwards. In this tent, the fortune teller, surrounded by the other women and children, sits cross-legged, her eyes sparkle out of a face that has played a thousand tricks.

Right: Gypsy families camp near the salt flats of Messolonghi and cook in their tents.

Left: Avgotaracho *(pressed grey mullet roe) is an expensive delicacy served thinly sliced with toast and lemon juice.*

Below: *Marcos Katsaros sells wild artichokes from his three-wheeler in Messolonghi and prepares them all day long in his tiny courtyard.*

Nothing can stop the simple disappearing trick, once it has started, that she plays with her hands and eyes, the 5,000 drachmae note that matches her one placed in the dirt, that miraculously disappears into the dirt. The illusion is so fast and the cackling, triumphant laugh so loud as the innocent leave the camp never to return again.

Messolonghi (or Missalonghi) does not dwell on past glory. There are no Bryon memorabilia shops living off his fatal stay in the town, helping organize the resistance against the Turks in the War of Independence, although there is a statue commemorating his death by fever and a small museum with some of his belongings.

Instead, it is a shabby town of celebration, that survives on the good fishing in the lagoon. The fishermen's huts stand on stilts in the lagoon, besides the various methods they use – the nets, traps and flat boats. *Tsipouro* (gilt-head bream), *lavraki* (sea bass) and *kefalos* (grey mullet) are caught in the labyrinth of traps. Large grey mullet are hightly prized and the eggs of the female are used to make the delicacy, *avgotaracho*.

This is made all over the Mediterranean in Egypt, Turkey, Tunisia, France (where it is called *poutargue*) and Italy (*bottarga*). Between August and September, the eggs are salted intact for five to six hours, washed and then dried in the sun and covered in beeswax. The pressed roes are very dear now, and are mostly sold only in expensive delicatessens in Athens; none ever seems to be available in the town itself. *Avgotaracho* is eaten in a *meze* in the homes of the old moneyed Athenians, thinly sliced with toast and lemon juice. Its strong flavour makes it a very good accompaniment to ouzo.

The town may be famous for its *avgotaracho*, but in May there is a far more exciting sight. Marcos Katsaros cycles his three-wheeler around

Left: An old pair of scissors ready to trim a basket of wild artichokes.

Right: Flowers are always kept in pots or painted olive oil cans on window sills.

the squares in the early evening, shouting 'Agroules, agroules' – wild artichoke hearts, that are only available at this time of year, sold in paper bags with little packages of salt, that everyone eats in the *ouzerie* and *kafeneia*. The tiny hearts are revealed after throwing away the outer leaves. He has been selling them for fifty-five years and in May, goes up to the slopes of Mount Arachinthos every day to collect them in the early morning. In the small courtyard of his house, the process of cleaning and trimming, boiling them in water with flat stones on top in old olive tin cans over primitive paraffin fires and packing them into bags, takes all day. The rewards are not great; calloused cut hands and a wife with a bad heart that keeps them both worried. All that keeps him going is his pleasure in making a humble living from this wild food that so many of the town enjoy. That, and the signed circular letters from the ex-King Constantine, thanking him for the Easter and Christmas cards he sends every year. 'The agroules grow all over the Peloponnese but nobody bothers with them the way I do' he says. 'And they are good for the liver, kidneys and for reducing fever.'

The town is a maze of narrow backstreets around the main square. At night it is packed with tables where the lightbulbs are strung along on precarious wires, and everyone seems to be eating *mezedes* from the lagoon, eating eel, fried, smoked or in stews, small crabs grilled *sta karvouna*, tiny prawns and *barbounakia* (small red mullet), or drinking small carafes of ouzo or bottles of local wine from Patras. There is often a small boy, given a few coins to run after the three-wheeler and that echoing cry of 'Agroules, agroules', as Costas cycles home for the night in time to be in the hills at 5am again.

In Galaxidi, the familiar Greece of caiques at the quayside, with names like 'Aphrodite' and 'Agios Andreas', and a salty scent of sea is a relief after the stagnant, mosquito-infested lagoons of western Roumeli. Galaxidi, once home of rich sea merchants, with its natural deep-water harbours on the gulf of Corinth, revels in its nautical

history. There is the museum which is a paean to the old sailing ships of the town, built in its shipyards in the early nineteenth century. Brazzera's, brigs, barquentines and schooners that travelled the Mediterranean and Black Sea as freight charters, bringing wealth and the big mansions. Some of these have been turned into intimate hotels like the Pensione Ganimede. This has a very good breakfast, with its homemade jams and free range eggs, served amidst the scented flowers of its courtyard. The Themistoklis *kafeneon* on the quay, no longer full of garrulous sea captains but their humble descendants who supply fresh fish to the restaurants next door, is the perfect setting for realizing that Greece is as much an idea as a country.

This is a place of different mountain and sea faring people, whose lifestyles are always dictated by the geography of the regions. If there is any sense of regional cuisine in Greece, it is governed by these factors, and always found in the simple kitchens of the villages. The true spirit of the mainland is also there and cannot be found by the tour-buses, in nearby Delphi, searching incessantly for irrelevant clues in the temples of ancient Greece.

Autumn/Winter Salad 'Mainland Style'

Cabbage and carrot salad

SERVES 2-4

½ white cabbage, very finely shredded
2 carrots, peeled and grated
30 ml/2 tbsp olive oil
juice of 1 lemon
salt and freshly ground black pepper

Place the shredded cabbage in a shallow bowl and put the grated carrots on top. Dribble olive oil and lemon juice on top and finally add salt and pepper.

Spanakorizzo

Spinach rice

This is also made with leeks or cabbage.

SERVES 4

1 large onion, or 5 spring onions (scallions), chopped
60 ml/4 tbsp olive oil
450 g/1 lb spinach, washed and roughly chopped
115 g/4 oz/⅔ cup long-grain white rice
15 ml/1 tbsp chopped fresh dill
salt and freshly ground black pepper
1.75 litres/3 pints/7½ cups water
lemon juice (optional)

In a large saucepan, sauté the onion in olive oil for 5 minutes, then add the spinach and stir until the spinach wilts. Add the rice, dill and seasoning. Cover with the water and simmer, partly covered, until the rice is cooked, stirring occasionally.

Place a clean cloth over the saucepan, replace the lid and leave until all the liquid has been absorbed. Serve warm, with a squeeze of lemon juice added, if desired.

Hirino Me Prassa

Pork and leeks

Winter stews of pork are also traditionally combined with *selino* (celery) or *andidia* (curly endive) with *avgolemono*.

SERVES 4

75-90 ml/5-6 tbsp olive oil
1 medium-sized onion, chopped
900 g/2 lb lean boneless pork, cubed
350 ml/12 fl oz/1½ cups water
30-45 ml/2-3 tbsp finely chopped celery leaves
or fresh flat-leafed parsley
salt and freshly ground black pepper
700 g/1½ lb leeks, cut into pieces

Heat the olive oil in a large saucepan, add the onion and brown the meat for 5 minutes. Then add the water, celery leaves or flat-leaved parsley and salt and pepper to taste, cover and cook for 45 minutes on a medium heat, stirring occasionally.

Add the leeks and mix in with the meat. Cook for a further 15 minutes until the meat is tender and sauce thickened.

Hirino me Prassa *(pork and leek stew).*

Soutzoukakia

Smyrna Sausages with cracked green olives

SERVES 4-6
2 Slices of bread, crustless
2 cloves garlic, peeled
10 ml/2 tsp ground cumin powder or crushed seeds
450 g/1 lb lean minced (ground) beef
1 egg, lightly beaten
salt and freshly ground black pepper
45 ml/3 tbsp olive oil or butter, or a mixture of the two
45 ml/3 tbsp white wine
450 g/1 lb ripe tomatoes, skinned and chopped large
handful of cracked green olives (do not substitute with Spanish green olives but use black olives if necessary)

Preheat the oven to 180°C/350°F/Gas Mark 4. Soak the bread in water for 15 minutes, then squeeze out excess moisture. Pound the garlic cloves and mix with the cumin. In a mixing bowl, combine the beef, bread, garlic and cumin, egg and seasoning. Blend thoroughly to make a thick paste.

Shape into oval 'sausages' and brown in the oil or butter in a frying pan for 5 minutes. Put the sausages in an ovenproofdish.

Add the wine to the frying pan and heat for a few minutes, then add the tomatoes and simmer for 5 minutes. Pour this mixture over the *soutzoukakia*.

Rinse the cracked olives and immerse in boiling water, then drain. Add to the dish around the sausages. Bake in the oven for 30 minutes. Serve with boiled rice.

Briam

Baked vegetable stew

The Greek 'ratatouille'. *Briam* always uses courgettes (zucchini), whereas *Tourlou*, another variation of Turkish origin, tends to use aubergines (eggplants) as well. The dish is always better lukewarm, and if served with *feta* and bread it makes a perfect summer lunch dish.

SERVES 4
75-90 ml/5-6 tbsp olive oil
2 medium-sliced onions, thickly sliced
450 g/1 lb courgettes (zucchini), peeled and thickly sliced
450 g/1 lb potatoes, peeled and thickly sliced or quartered
4 large ripe tomatoes, thickly sliced
1/2 green sweet pepper, thickly sliced (optimal)
15 ml/1 tbsp tomato paste, dissolved in 175 ml/6 fl oz/3/4 cup hot water
45 ml/3 tbsp finely chopped fresh flat-leafed parsley
salt and freshly ground black pepper

Preheat the oven to 180°C/350°F/Gas Mark 4.

Heat 45 ml/3 tbsp olive oil in a pan and sauté the onions for 5 minutes. In a large *tapsi* or oven-proof dish, place the courgettes (zucchini), potatoes, tomatoes and green pepper, if using, mixing them evenly. Add the onions and tomato paste mixture. Sprinkle parsley, salt, black pepper and the rest of the olive oil.

Cover with foil and bake in the oven for 1½ hours. Remove the foil for the last 30 minutes of cooking, to allow the top to brown, and add a little more liquid if needed. Allow to cool and then serve.

Spetsofai

Sausage and green pepper stew

This dish is only really authentic if strong coarse sausages and thin sweet peppers are used as in Pelion where they also sometimes substitute dried red peppers. Many cooks leave the tomatoes or paste out of the dish for a more basic flavour.

SERVES 4
450 g/1 lb pale green, long sweet peppers, cored and thickly sliced
45 ml/3 tbsp olive oil

450 g/1 lb coarse country sausages, sliced in 1 cm/½ inch thick pieces
1 large ripe tomato, skinned and chopped, or 7.5 ml/½ tbsp tomato paste diluted in 60 ml/4 tbsp water
salt and freshly ground black pepper
15 ml/1 tbsp dried oregano (optional)

Sauté the peppers in 30 ml/2 tbsp of the olive oil in a frying pan. Fry the sausages in another pan in the remaining oil for 5 minutes. Add them to the peppers with the tomato or tomato paste mixture. Add seasoning and the oregano, if using, and stir. Cover and cook on a low heat for 20 minutes until the sauce reduces.

Spetsofai, fasolia *and* galotyri, *specialities of Mount Pelion.*

The City

'When you drink in the taverna, you sit and don't speak, now and then you sigh from the depths of your heart.'

from a *rembetiko* song by
Tsitsanis

The city is never quiet, always restless like its impatient inhabitants on the crowded buses, trying to share taxis or cramming into the metro line that takes everyone into offices from the suburbs. From the semi-slums of Piraeus to Kifissia with its neo-classical villas and shopping malls, narcissistic Kolonaki and crumbling Plaka, the Athenians are waking to another day of chaotic working ritual. For those who come to see the golden city of ancient learning, the classicism is covered in a layer of grime from the *nefos*, the cloud of pollution that hangs in retribution on overcast days; or surrounded by scaffolding in a permanent state of repair. Like the fool on the hill, the Acropolis stands in immovable stony silence, waiting for the tourists to go home. For them, the city is often a disappointment, an ugly farce of

Above: *The Aristokraton cake shop.* Left: *The Vlachika restaurants of Vari at night.*

unfinished apartment blocks and relentless heat in the summer months.

But for Athenians it is the spirit of the place that is important. Just as every Greek struggles with the notion of the homeland, especially the *emigrés* who cling to the image of the conservative village as spiritual home; so the modern Athenian, born and bred in the city, unties that knot and values a different kind of modern Hellenism. The Athenian has a love-hate relationship with the city that is both a symbol of old and new Greece and the search for liberty often explodes on the streets in the violence of rebellion (the student battle for the Polytechnic against the Colonels in November 1973, for example) or at any political rally. The simple affirmation of democratic values is omni-present in the *kafeneia* and restaurants in the everyday celebration of eating and drinking.

The Athenian is equally passionate about politics and *parea*, the enjoyment of food and drink with friends. The crowds that gather at the *periptera* to read the latest headlines of

Around Omonia Square, the street vendors sell late-night souvlaki and sandwiches.

the dozens of different daily newspapers, or in Omonia square (the equivalent of London's Speakers Corner) late at night to hear the demagogic rant of a union official, are always eating and drinking from the street stalls of Athinas street. They stay open all night making a special type of sandwich, filled with ham, cheese, tomato and hot skewers of *souvlaki*.

Three events irrevocably changed the eating habits of the city: the sack of Smyrna in 1922 and the exchange of populations between Turkey and Greece bringing 1½ million refugees into the country; the opening of the first fast-food outlet, called the Royale in 1969, and Greece's entrance into the EEC in 1981. The sophistication of the refugees, who were settled in areas of Piraeus like Drapetsona or new suburbs like Nea Ionia, Nea Smyrni and Kessariani, brought new Eastern influences into mainstream life. The cosmopolitan café lifestyle of the rich and *tekés* (hashish dens) of the poor refugees, slowly infiltrated into the mainstream through their *rembetika* music and Turkish names for the food they liked to eat like *fasolia piaz* and *yaourtlou*.

Hamburgers hit Athens in 1969 when the Royale opened in Glyfada, and, although it is still one of the few cities to be without an official McDonald's outlet, they are available at every snack bar in the city. After the *tiropitta* and *loukanopitta* (sausage roll) they are probably the most popular street food. At the famous Everest in Kolonaki, the art of the snack reaches new heights. The *tost* of the town is made with combinations of over twenty fillings. Two 'chefs' slap hamburgers, ham, bacon and *kapnisto* (smoked pork chops) onto the grills, splitting open the bread rolls and spooning egg mayonnaise or Russian salad, tomatoes or raw onion to await the meat and are then toasted quickly while the customer queues to pay for his selection at the counter.

When Greece joined the Common Market, products began to flood the shops, often cheaper than local foodstuffs and the slow homogenization into the western European style

has only really just begun. The new woman (for they still do most of the cooking) who read recently-launched versions of Greek *Elle* and *Marie Claire*, buy European products from supermarkets like Vassilopoulos and are more likely to experiment with French cuisine at dinner parties, leaving the Greek food to the tavernas and the male chefs who instinctively stick to the ancient rhythms and beats of the recipes that they know best.

Beneath the Acropolis, early morning life is little changed. In the Anafiotika area, where workers from Anafi built their houses in the Cycladic style, cats bask on the roof-tops and a woman paints the road with whitewash. An arthritic man is returning home from the bakery with the morning bread. In every area of Athens, the village mentality still struggles to survive with the small specialist shops that people like to visit. In Plateia Iroon, close to Athinas street, it is like an island square with its tavernas and *kafeneon*, basement general store and a cheese shop that only sells *graviera* and *mezithra* from Naxos.

Despite the growth of smart shops likes Precieux in Akadimias street which stocks Fauchon goods or Cellier in Kriestotou which has

Right: *Some tavernas specialize in grilled or stewed eel, crabs and prawns.*

*Old wine-shops are found
throughout the city.*

Fortnum & Mason hampers, Athens is still a city of local markets that set up in the street on alternate weekdays in different areas like Kolonaki or Kefalari. On Sundays, there is always the flea-market of Monastiraki or Piraeus where the food stalls are out-numbered by the bric-à-brac and black market caviar sold by Poles and Russians who work in the city illegally. They can be bargained down to absurdly low prices.

But it is Athinas street and the enclosed *Kentriki Agora* that is busiest every morning. Generally 30 per cent cheaper than elsewhere, the covered galleries of the meat and fish market, and the fruit and vegetable market opposite, are always crowded. Everything for the kitchen and home can be bought in the surrounding streets. There are shops selling kitchen safes, mousetraps and olive oil cans and funnels.

Above: *The busy fish section of Athinas market has small passageways with tiny bars where the stallholders eat and drink.*
Right top: *Herb shops abound with their cures for almost any illness.*
Right bottom: *Olives and pickles are sold loose by the kilo.*

The religious shops where beeswax candles of different sizes are weighed and sold by the kilo stand among the icons and incense. In alleys off Ermou street and around Plateia Iroon, there are kitchen shops with *tapsia* for the oven; *flitzanakia* (the solid-handled *metrio* cups); small ouzo glasses; metal aluminium wine measures; *kafeneon* trays for waiters to hold from the handle as they weave along the street to offices who have ordered coffee, even cups and saucers with the political symbols of PASOK and KKE (the communist party).

There are basements that just have wooden chopping boards and stamps for religious bread,

knives and graters or the cheese shop Zafolia in Evripidou street that sells 150 barrels of *feta* every three days. Sofokleos is the street for herbs at Dafnoula where a huge bulb hangs next to a sign saying 'It's good for halting hair loss', and the barrels and baskets are filled with herbs and teas. 'Leaves of Egypt' for constipation, *molocha* for colds, oregano, mint and thyme. In Sokratou street, the two old *ladadika* (olive shops) sit over a basement taverna which serves basic food. The Papalexandris store, opened in 1921, sells over twenty-five varieties of olives from huge plastic barrels. *Throumbes* from Thassos and *analates throumbes* (unsalted olives) from

Imported sides of salt cod.

Crete, *tsakistes* (cracked green olives) from Attika, large fleshy olives from Amfissa and Agrinio, small jet-black olives from Kalamata and Arachova, are all sold by weight, the minimum is always one kilo. There are also different types of pickles, large tins of anchovies and sardines from Mitilini.

Down Armadiou street, the *horta* stalls sell *italika* a type of *radikia* and other greens; the meat stores have *pastourma kapnisto* hams, sausages with leek and coarse black sausages for *spetsofai*. Children always have to be pulled away from Dimitris Paraskevipoulos' shop of live birds like partridges, quail, even turkeys crouch sullenly in their cages next to the rabbits. Pulse shops display their lentils, split-peas for *fava*, beans from Prespa and Kastoria, dried and wrinkled *koukia* (broad beans), different kinds of rice in sacks and barrels; nuts from Aegina, stuffed *syka* (figs) from Evia, marbled *halva* flavoured with chocolate or almond waits to be sliced, bottles of *soumada* (almond syrup) and *vissinada* (cherry syrup) from Aegina are at the sweet stands.

The oldest businesses are the Polidi *kafeneon* (open since 1919) in Aionou down marble stairs to a basement of worn red floor-tiles and three-legged metal tables where a *meze* is still given with the ouzo, and the *potopieon* (wine

shop) called Finopoulou, on the corner of Evripidou and Athinas. Dusty bottles of brandy, liqueurs and Mavrodaphne wine opposite the booth where metal tokens are bought and presented to the barmen who dispense a strong shot of *raki* or *mastika*, gulped down in one. These are places still frequented by the market men just starting or finishing work.

Close-by in Monastiraki and Plaka, the tavernas are busy at lunchtime. In the *kafeneon* 'i Oraia Ellas' ('beautiful Greece') in the crafts centre in Mitropoleos street, two brothers make popular *pikilia* (a selection of hot and cold *mezedes*) amidst framed political cartoons and the naïve work of the artist, Themis Tsironis.

In Plateia Abbyssinia, the three-wheelers come in on Saturday mornings with the occasional antique amidst the junk. There is an auction room where bad oil paintings are sold and next door, Abbyssinia, a six-tabled narrow bar that serves *feta* baked with paprika, *manitaria me skordo* (mushrooms with garlic) and ice-cold draught Amstel beer. In and around Plaka's main square, Costis, Psaras and Tsekouras are tavernas known to most Athenians; for locals they are places for *parea*, where friends are always likely to be at lunchtime. Costis has good

Sandwich sellers make mid-morning snacks for city workers.

The Finopoulou, next to Athinas market, serves shots of ouzo *and* mastika *to regulars.*

yiouvarlakia (rice meat balls), *soupies me spanaki* (cuttlefish and spinach) and *fasolia* examined in the kitchen by newcomers who know nothing about the unchanging menu. At Psaras, it is the shade of the tree-lined square and sloping tables as much as the food, courgettes (zucchini), grilled *soupies* or *kalamari* and *xiphias* (swordfish), that keep it busy in summer. Tsekouras has its indoor fig-tree and is opposite the *kafeneon* with an open-fire in winter. Plaka is full of such places visited in rotation on a daily basis by people who hardly ever cook at home.

The Athenians eat at all hours. Those that start work early at 8am usually have lunch at 1pm, those that begin later will have lunch from 3pm onwards and everyone survives on the streetsnacks like *koulouria* or *tiropittes* if they have no time at all; sold from small stands with drawers filled with sandwich ingredients, sliced tomatoes, cheese, sesame rolls.

Throughout the winter, indoor restaurants like Kentrikon and Ideal are busier; in summer, anywhere outdoors like Manessis in Metz or Balthasar's, in Kolonaki, a crowded garden bar; food becomes secondary to the obsession with eating outdoors. There are smart expense account establishments like Gerofinikas or Je Reviens, the new Pentelikon hotel or the Hilton's restaurants that are usually a disappointment to people who yearn for the humble food of the tavernas. Eating expensive, second-rate French food like *coq au vin* or *escargots* ten years after they were fashionable in Je Reviens is a depressing example of the old snobbery of the rich Athenians who still dress up in their suits and fur coats for dinner. At Gerofinikas, which is always recommended by Greeks as the best restaurant in town, by which they mean the most expensive, the food is as bad as the kitsch surroundings. Waiters in shiny blue or ochre dinner jackets, who seem to have learnt their trade on too many summer cruise ships, place the flag of your nationality on the table (that can be confusing with mixed parties) and then reel off the specialities like *mouskari en papillote*, or lobster with cheese, before even mentioning a few Greek dishes like *fricassé* and *kolokithia*. It is a place to avoid, whatever its reputation might have been, if only because it shows one of the reasons why Greek food never succeeds in smart surroundings when its true spirit is found in tavernas with natural atmosphere and unpretentious food.

Even the new wave restaurants that Athenians find so fashionable, and opened by a younger generation who have travelled, like Ratga's (or Montparnasse as it is also called) in Kolonaki, Symposio in Erechthiou street beneath the Acropolis, or 1900 at Solonos and Sina streets, show how misguided attempts at modern European cuisine usually are. Dishes look as though they have been found in the pages of old cookery magazines and are distant memories for many of us, like deep-fried camembert or mushrooms, salads of apple and celery, spinach, bacon and croûton salads or dwarf corn. Ratga's

Basement tavernas around Plaka Square specialize in bakaliaros me skordalia *(salt-cod and garlic sauce) during the Lenten fasting.*

is still the smart drinking haunt for the Kolonaki crowd. Symposio and 1900 try harder to adapt Greek food into a lighter formula. Symposio is in a restored neo-classical house and garden, and offers Greek 'nouvelle cuisine', not something that bears thinking about, no rich olive oil to dip bread into or heavy warming pulses but 'light' dishes like *pestrofa* (smoked trout) or *midia* (mussels). But the setting in summer, beneath a huge palm tree, makes it almost worthwhile. The 1900 restaurant Café Estiatorio is another clever conversion that allows the light to come in through a glass roof. It too roots itself in the early 1980s with dishes like *soufflé anginares* (artichoke soufflé), smoked chicken and tartare sauce, it is only with its Greek *mezedes* like *kasseropita* (cheese pie), *sikotakia ladorigani* (chopped liver with oil and oregano sauce), *kremmidia gemista* (stuffed onions), *doma-tokeftedes* (tomato rissoles) and *hortokeftedes* (spinach rissoles) that it succeeds in going back

to the roots of Greek cuisine. Any attempts at new Greek food, meaning hip, always fail. It is not made for adaptation but for adherence to and like most peasant cuisine needs no changing. Even the Spaniards, who have nine different regional cuisines to work with and much stronger gastronomic traditions, fail with their attempts at *nueva cucina*.

The search for traditional *estiatoria* (restaurants), *psarotavernes* (fish tavernas), *psistaries* (meat restaurants), *ouzerie*, *mezedopoleion* and tavernas that offer real Greek food in Athens is not difficult. They are all around, it is just that the new Greeks often undervalue their own cuisine and, understandably, want something different which is why the few Chinese, Japanese and Italian restaurants do so well.

First, there are the central restaurants like Ideal in Panepistimiou street or Kentrikon in Kolokotroni street, both of which are old favourites with all Athenians. They are not places

Anginares a la Polita *(Artichokes in the Constantinople style) and antique copper ouzo carafes and glasses.*

for *parea* or serious enjoyment and political argument but rather they are the places to meet elderly aunts and uncles. They are fast restaurants with many tables and waiters that are busy all afternoon with regulars.

Ideal, with its refrigerated window display of fish set into the wall, is easy to miss in the lunchtime crowds walking between Syntagma and Omonia squares. There is no atmosphere but efficiency. It is the food that counts, perfectly fried *melitzanes* (aubergines [egpplants]) or *kolokythia tiganita* (fried courgettes [zucchini]) with *skordalia*, *taramokeftedes* (cod roe rissoles), the obligatory plates of *horta*, the *soutzoukakia* and *pastitsio*, and the ice-cold bottles of wine. Most people eat quickly, quietly. There always seems to be a table of priests and lawyers, mothers with their daughters and the odd tourist couple in their shorts.

Kentrikon seems less hectic, the pace dictated by many regulars, solitary men who are in no hurry. On their civil service pensions they survive the recent and rapid changes in the cost of living, by reading the paper all afternoon at their usual tables. The restaurant does certain seasonal dishes very well like *anginares à la Polita* (artichokes in the Constantinople style),

kotopoulo me purée (roast chicken with puréed potato) and *fakes* (lentil soup). In the strange world of 1960s' panelled wood and hanging cinema foyer lighting, it is an old-fashioned, curiously Athenian restaurant that provides nursery food for the faithful.

Then there are the *ouzerie mezedopoleion* in the centre, Apotsos, Athinaikion, Mytilini and Paradosiako, where everything always seems more animated and relaxed. Like the big, selection of *mezedes* that come fast and furious, the conversation twists and turns; rooms are smoky, loud and crowded.

At Apotsos, in Panepistimiou street, tucked down an alley, the haunt of politicians from the nearby parliament, is a high-ceilinged, sparse room. The only decoration are the old advertising posters for shipping and import/export agencies. Together with the nearby cake shop, Aristokratikon in Voukourestiou street and Zonars, the café in Panepistimiou, they are landmarks from the heyday of high society Athens. In Zonars, the time warp continues for the elderly men and women drinking their 'café au lait' or hot chocolate.

The city is full of arcades with hidden *ouzerie* like Paradasiako, in Ippokratous street opposite the National Library. A black and white Greek Tourist Board photograph of a caique and the sea, and a model wooden galleon are the icons to the Aegean, the votive offering dishes like *gavros* (anchovies) *octapodi marinato, midia saganaki* (mussels baked in a 'saganaki' pan), *fasolia plaki*, fried *goppes* (like whitebait) and *lakerda*. The ouzo comes in small bottles, brands like 12, Sans Rival and Mini from Mitilini.

In Themistokleos street, off Omonia square, two *ouzerie* compete for business. Athanaikon specializes in *ameletita* – offal *mezedes* like *miala* (fried brains), *glossa lemonati* (tongue), *spetsofai* and forty other dishes; Mytilini, in a tiny alley opposite a faded *kafeneon*, in fish and seafood. The octopuses are handing on a line next to the charcoal grill, crushed ice keeps the small plates of *kochilia* and *stridia* (oysters) chilled, fried *marides* (picarel) are ordered with carafes of ouzo. This is a working-class *ouzerie* whose fame has spread; the tables and conversation crowd into the street as three small gypsy boys play violin, clarinet and drums to the students and lawyers who come from nearby Exarchia square, where the lawyers have their offices and the students, who used to like being anarchists and communists, discuss politics in the outdoor cafés.

Despite the brief popularity of the Piano Bar and Bistro in the late 1970s and early 1980s, this is still a democratic society not burdened by the snobbery of élitist eating. Everyone eats in the humble taverna. It is as important a symbol to the Greek way of life as the pub or bar are in Britain and America. Even the bastardization of Greek social culture cannot threaten its existence.

Taverna names also indicate the very social art of eating and drinking in Greece. Common names like 'Steki' (meeting place), 'Ta Tria Adelfia' ('The three brothers'), 'Tou Hondrou' ('the fat one') and 'O Glaros' ('the seagull') are recurring names that immediately identify the type of taverna through historical and social association. 'To steki tis Elenas', literally 'Eleni's meeting place' where the *parea* centres around the owner's personality; 'Ta Tria Adelfia', a family run taverna that will always serve reliable family food; 'Tou Hondrou' is the meat restaurant for feasting and overeating; 'O Glaros' the fish taverna that offers the frugal fruits of the sea.

Even for the new generation in the city, who grow up on fast food, pizza, spaghetti, hamburgers and over-doting Greek mothers who feed them traditional home cooking, these tavernas play a dominant role in the formality of ritual Greek eating.

In Athens, tavernas are also visited by area. People go to the garden tavernas of Kifissia in the summer when that suburb is noticeably cooler and, for the same reasons, to the fish tavernas of Piraeus and the coast. These tavernas tend to have identifiable decoration, the simplistic imagery of the sea, a few nets strung across the roof, stuffed fish, dried octopus, shells and model caiques.

In Kesseriani, one of the resettlement areas for refugees from Asia Minor in 1922, and a subsequent hot-bed for communism, the fish restaurants in the square are like this. Unpretentious places with panelled wood rooms upstairs where the waiters bring trays of *karavides* (langoustines) or *kalamarakia sta karvouna* (charcoal grilled squid), *garides giouvetsi* (prawns baked with feta and tomato), *atherina* (fried smelt) and fresh fruit to end the meal.

The fish restaurants of Tourkolimano are potent symbols, notorious from countless backdrops in 1960's Greek movies, of the high life. The clichés of those comic films (starring national heros like Nicos Rizos, Lambros Konstandaras and Aliki Vouyouklaki) about *mangas* (gangsters) and their molls, gullible American tourists and stupid police inspectors, keep the harbour alive. It is as expensive as ever yet no one seems to mind paying the prices. To sit in a small harbour of fishing boats after work, with a *bouzouki* player by the table and a gypsy girl selling roses, is romance enough for many Athenians. A simple meal of *garidosoupa*

Bananas are sold to passengers boarding the early morning ferries at Piraeus.

(prawn and tomato soup) and one plainly grilled *fagri* (sea bream), *horiatiki* salad and a bottle of *retsina* can be the perfect meal. Anything more and the credit cards are needed.

Meat restaurants, or *psistaria*, also have their own mountain imagery from the mainland; copper pots, shepherds' crooks and thick rugs pinned on the walls, open fires and winter stoves, photographs from the Epirot homeland. The Vlachika restaurants in Vari, behind Voula on the coast, put up the Christmas decorations at Christmas, the coloured lights strung across the road and on the Christmas trees. In a way, everyday is like the Easter celebrations in these restaurants where the lamb, goat and *kokkoretsi* (grilled offal) turn continously on spits, *gouronopoulo* (roast sucking pig) in the oven and *paidakia* (lamb chops) ready for cooking, all sold by weight. Charcoal, that great despoiler of the forests in ancient Greece when the towns clamoured for more and more of it for their cooking, sits in bags by the large spit.

Fried courgettes (zucchini) or aubergines (eggplants) and thin sauté potatoes with grated cheese accompany the meat and yoghurt with honey is always offered at the end of the meal. Nowadays, Lebanese who have fled Beirut are the main lunchtime customers and come for one of the specialities, roasted sheep's head cut in two to facilitate eating. Bad Greek music gives a continuous carnival feel and the antics of the *kraktes* ('crows'), the men in long butcher's aprons who stop the cars that pass by, urging the drivers into their restaurants. Forcing the innocent into the world of carnal delights offered by the restaurants called 'The Net of the Hunter', 'Uncle Tom's Cabin', 'Vaskopoula' and 'Vlachika'.

There is another kind of special meat restaurant in Athens, more low-life atmosphere from a noted working-class area. In 1922, poor refugees hit Drapetsona, on the hill behind the port of Piraeus and soon set up their own restaurants which still survive around Sokratous street, serving the best kebabs in the city, food for those nostalgic for Asia Minor. Only open at night for *souvlakia tis Drapetsonas* from 6pm until 2am, these beer and *souvlaki* joints make a special kind of *kembab* (*souvlaki*) or *soutzouki* (a skewer of flattened minced meat). Pitta is grilled, chopped and laid on a plate, the meat is skewered on top with grilled tomatoes, chopped onions and parsley. The formula has not changed since the 1920s. *Tzatziki*, chips and beer are the only accompaniment to these filling kebabs. At Abraam and Karababas, the waiters carry trays of the kebabs to adjoining dining rooms along the street. Opposite in the *periptero*, the woman is always watching these cheerful waiters as they take the empty plates back. The kebab houses that have infiltratred the British high street could learn something from these masters of the art of unadorned kebab-making.

Late at night, the city begins to stir. People who have returned home, start to telephone friends to see which taverna to meet in. Eating begins late: from 10pm, tavernas fill; before 8pm many are too busy preparing food to allow anyone in. Around Kolonaki and Lykabettos, Metz and Plaka are some of the best neighbourhood tavernas, if one is full the next one is visited. Even in sophisticated Kolonaki with its expensive fashion and interior design shops, the

In Drapetsona, near the docks in Piraeus, refugees from Smyrna sell the best kebabs in the city.

A typical neighbourhood restaurant, Vlassis in Lykabettos, where the waiter brings a tray loaded with starters.

tavernas are mercifully run-down. Rodia, in Aristippou, with its quiet garden and Dimocritou, usually busy with assistants from the fashion shops in Tsakalof street, where the fast service and reliable seasonal food, dishes like *moschari me kidonia* (beef with quinces), *kreatosoupa* (beef and vegetable stew) for the infirm, *horta* and a very good *fricassée* (lamb and lettuce stew), make it the place for a quick meal before hitting the nearby bars.

Then, there is Vlassis in Argyroupoleos street beneath Lykabettos, one of the classic neighbourhood tavernas for a longer evening of *parea*, serious eating and drinking. Locals are in there every night, the food changes daily but there are always favourite dishes, brought on a large wooden tray to the table to start the meal off. *Kounoupidi* (boiled cauliflower), *tsirosalmas* (chopped liver with bechamel and cheese), *bakaliaros* (salt cod with hot chilli peppers), *piperies tiganites* (fried peppers), *patsaria me skordalia* (beetroot with garlic) and

fava. The fresh fish usually disappears early but the roasts remain, *gourounopoulo* (suckling pig) or *arni sto fourno* (lamb), both served with potatoes and mustard. The owner, Vlassis, comes with the bill; there are people waiting in the street and the noisy group by the door are demanding more wine. The art gallery posters on the walls, the only testimony that counts from the loyal customers.

There are smarter establishments like Okio, in Haritos street in Kolonaki, with its authentic northern dishes like *prassopittes* (leek pies), *biftekia gemista me tiri* (beef stuffed with cheese), or Saamandra in Mantzarou, with its large selection of *saganakia* (fried cheeses), where the food is excellent but somehow their formal atmosphere jar in the chaos of true Athenian eating.

At night, the bar-life of the city drags on into the early hours and continues in the *rembetika* clubs and discotheques. Around Exarchia square, every restored neo-classical building seems to be a bar serving *sfinakia*, shooters, the small lethal liqueur mixes, the latest cocktail craze in the city. There are new wave bars opening all over the city, that emulate the west far better than the foreign restaurants. Open mostly in the winter, some survive the initial costs of setting up to become the 'in' bar of the season, others struggle on until the summer when the owners return to their lucrative island bars in Santorini and Ios. Some like Tounta's in Lykabettos, which is an art gallery as well, give a slick vision of the new Greece of efficiency and overwhelming trendiness.

Others, like Loras in Plateia Mavili, offer the warmth of the old Greece. This dark and cramped bar near the American Embassy, run by smiling Loras who can never leave the bar, attracts everyone. In summer, the bikes park outside and become impromtu tables and chairs for the beer bottles and in winter, the regulars huddle inside with their whisky and sodas. Loras remembers everyone's birthday or the birth of a new Greek as if it were affirmation

Athens is still a city of back streets where old men find the time to play tavli *(backgammon).*

of the Athenian's will to survive. Everyone in the bar is bought a round of drinks, the door is closed as the singing begins.

It is through *kefi*, the abandonment of self through drink for a few hours, that people survive the city. In the *rembetika* clubs, friends drink to dance, with sorrow and joy. *Rembetika* music remains a cathartic experience for all Greeks. Like Portuguese *fado* or the American blues, it comes out of the suffering of the poor. Originally the music of the refugees from Asia Minor, the petty criminals and prostitutes of waterfront Piraeus, who smoked hashish and spent most of their time in jail, it was a spontaneous cry against their suffering. Like the blues, the songs are mostly about unrequited love or the search for a decent way of life. Today, recognized by all sections of society as a potent, unique form of Greek expression, *rembetika* becomes a cry for freedom.

The new city Greeks, at clubs like Esmeralda in Kefalinias street or Taximi in Harilaou Tri-ekoupi, reveal the strangely spiritual power that everyday living still has in Greece. Because of the suffering and turmoil of recent history universally felt to a greater degree in the city the Greeks can celebrate in a way that other city-dwellers cannot and *rembetika* is the best

emotional therapy for its practitioners.

At Taximi, the young band play on a raised platform like their idols, Vasilis Tsitsanis and Sotiria Bellou, playing *bouzouki*, *baklamas*, violin and *santouri*, the classical songs requested by the student crowd. A boy with long hair and cowboy boots dances the solitary *zembekiko*, a cigarette dangling from his mouth like an old-time *mangas*.

Afterwards, people go to Athinas market and the 24-hour tavernas. The only time they ever close is on Sunday night for they are always packed with the most democratic cross-section of inhabitants in the city. Before dawn, it is the turn of the revellers who come, elated from the clubs, to the empty enclosed meat market of the *Kentriki agora*. The butcher's shutters are still down and the chopping boards scrubbed clean for the morning business, when the chic Kolonaki crowd arrive in their Japanese designer clothes. A *bekris* (drunk) is slumped on the marble top table. Behind the long counter is ever classic dish, the nourishing bean soups, *stifado* (stews), pasta, *horta* and salty blocks of *feta*, *lachanodolmades* and steaming pots of *patsas*, the tripe soup that is considered to be the best hangover food in the country, a warming restorative that has garlic-flavoured vinegar

One of the tavernas in Athinas market, that stay open 24-hours, and serve classic food like patsas *(tripe soup) and* fassolada *(bean soup).*

Brettos, in Plaka, sells its own label
mastika *and liqueurs.*

poured into it from the individual bottles at every table. The fishmongers, who start earlier, are already eating breakfast bowls of this soup and *skordalia*. A meal at the three market tavernas rejuvenates everyone, unconsciously they re-affirm all that is best about Greek food. There is as much a link with the past here as in the unchanged island taverna. Whatever the magpie origins of Greek food might be, with its Turkish, Venetian and ancient influences, it remains constant to the true spirit of Greek life in its simplicity. Even if in twenty years, the new generation have cooked their way around the recipes of Europe and dishes like *fasolia* and *patsas* were to become the joke food of Greece, these tavernas will still remain, waiting to be rediscovered by those who had stupidly abandoned their own culture and cuisine.

As dawn breaks, the *laiki agora* (markets) are setting up, piling high the *anginares* and *horta* for the wealthy in Kifissia and the poor in Piraeus. In the market tavernas there is a rare moment of peace as the market men rush to open their stalls. The waiters sit down for coffee and the sweating chef goes outside to smoke a cigarette in the sun. As the echoing cry of the stall holders begins, the widows in black arrive to buy the best of the early morning catch.

Anginares Me Koukia

Artichokes with fresh broad beans

SERVES 4

8 small globe artichokes, trimmed and halved
juice of 2 small lemons
75-90 ml/5-6 tbsp olive oil
8-10 shallots or small onions, peeled and left
whole
8 medium-sized potatoes, peeled and quartered,
or 6 new potatoes, peeled
450 g/1 lb fresh broad (fava) beans, shelled and
left whole
45 ml/3 tbsp chopped fresh dill
300 ml/½ pint/1¼ cups water
salt and freshly ground black pepper

Turn the artichokes by cutting off the tough
outer leaves and most of the stem. Leave 7.5 cm/
3 inches of stem and shave the rough outer skin
away. Slice through the upper leaves and dis-
card. Halve the artichokes and remove the
chokes. Rub lemon juice over the artichokes and
place in a bowl of acidic water (water and lemon
juice) to prevent discolouring.

Heat the olive oil in a saucepan, add the
shallots and potatoes and fry gently for 5
minutes. Add the artichokes with the remaining
ingredients and cover with the water. Simmer
gently for 1 hour or until the vegetables are
tender and the sauce has reduced. Serve gar-
nished with more chopped dill.

Garides Giouvetsi

Prawns with feta and tomato

This is a dish found at all the restaurants around
Tourkolimano in Piraeus. It is either baked or
fried.

60 ml/4 tbsp olive oil
2 garlic cloves, finely chopped (optional)
4 or 5 large tomatoes, skinned and coarsely
chopped
30 ml/2 tbsp finely chopped fresh flat-leafed
parsley
2 dried chilli peppers, seeded and broken up, or
1 fresh green sweet pepper, cored and sliced
(both optional)
700 g/1½ lb raw prawns (shrimp), thawed if
frozen
175 g/6 oz *feta* cheese, crumbled
salt and freshly ground black pepper

Preheat the oven to 200°C/400°F/Gas Mark 6, if
baking the dish.

Heat the olive oil in a large frying pan, add
the garlic, tomatoes, parsley and chilli or sweet
peppers (if using) and simmer for 10 minutes.
Then add the prawns (shrimp) and simmer for a
further 10 minutes. Season to taste.

If baking in an earthenware *giouvetsi* dish,
add the *feta*, transfer to the oven and bake for 15
minutes. Otherwise, add the *feta* to the pan and
continue to simmer for another 5 minutes until
the prawns (shrimp) are cooked.

Garides giouvesti *(baked prawns and feta).*

Pasteli

Sesame seed and honey sweets

Traditionally, these small wrapped pieces of pasteli are given at baptisms. Some versions add pistachios, walnuts or almonds. Use equal amounts of honey and sesame seeds and cook as for caramel to 'firm ball' stage using a sugar thermometer.

450 g/1 lb/1⅓ cups honey
175 ml/6 fl oz/¾ cup water
450 g/1 lb/3 cups sesame seeds
60 g/2 oz/½ cup blanched almonds, finely crushed
2 slices of orange zest, finely diced

In a heavy pan, bring the honey and water to 'firm ball stage' (130°C/250°F). Take off the heat and stir in the sesame seeds, almonds and orange zest. On a flat marble surface, or metal trays moistened with water, spread the mixture evenly with a spatula or knife to 1 cm/½ inch thickness. Before it cools, cut into squares. When it is cool, wrap the squares in waxed paper and store in a covered container.

Melitzanes Sto Fourno

Baked aubergines with cheese

SERVES 4-6
900 g/2 lb large aubergines (eggplants)
about 45 ml/3 tbsp olive oil
3 garlic cloves, finely sliced
4 large ripe tomatoes, skinned and coarsely chopped
15 ml/1 tbsp tomato paste, dissolved in 90 ml/6 tbsp water
45 ml/3 tbsp finely chopped fresh parsley

salt and freshly ground black pepper
115 g/4 oz hard cheese like *kefalotiri* (or Parmesan), grated

Peel the aubergines (eggplants) with a potato peeler, leaving stripes of skin, then cut into 1 cm/½ inch slices. Sprinkle with salt and allow to drain in a colander. Preheat the oven to 180°C/350°F/Gas Mark 4.

Heat the olive oil in a large frying pan. Squeeze the aubergine (eggplant) slices dry and then fry for 5 minutes or until they begin to brown, ading more oil to the pan if necessary. Drain on paper towels. Layer the slices in a large baking tin, *tapsi* or casserole dish.

In the frying pan, sauté the garlic and tomatoes, then add the tomato paste and mixture and cook until the liquid has evaporated. Season this mixture with the parsley, salt and pepper and pour over the aubergine (eggplant) slices. Dribble a little extra olive oil on top and then add the grated cheese. Bake for 30 minutes until browned on top.

Vissinada

Sour cherry preserve

1 kg/2 lb sour cherries
1 kg/2 lb/5 cups sugar
juice of 1 lemon, strained
350 ml/12 fl oz/1½ cups water

Wash and stone (pit) the cherries in a large bowl so that the juices are kept. Boil with the sugar, lemon juice and water in a heavy saucepan for about 20 minutes, skimming the scum off the top. When the syrup reaches setting point, allow to cool, then pour into sterilized glass jars. Store in a cool place and serve as *glyko koutaliou* to guests.

Yiouvarlakia

Rice and minced meatballs

This is usually made with *avgolemono* sauce added at the end. If it is eaten as a soup, vegetables like chopped carrots and celery are also added to thicken the sauce.

SERVES 4-6
900 g/2 lb minced (ground) beef
2 large onions, grated
75 g/2½ oz/½ cup rice
75-90 ml/5-6 tbsp finely chopped fresh flat-leafed parsley
30 ml/2 tbsp olive oil
salt and freshly ground black pepper
900 ml/1½ pts/3¾ cups water or stock
For *avgolemono* sauce:
juice of 1 lemon
2 eggs, lightly beaten

Mix the beef, onions, rice, parsley, oil and seasoning in a bowl, kneading together until blended and then roll into large walnut-sized balls. If these are too small or large they tend to break up, so it is important to get the size just right.

In a large saucepan bring the water or stock to the boil and then simmer. Add the *yiouvarlakia* slowly and pack tightly in two layers. The liquid should just cover them. Simmer, covered, for 30 minutes and then remove from the heat.

To make the *avoglemono* sauce, add the lemon juice to the beaten eggs in a bowl and stir. Then take 175 ml/6 fl oz/¾ cup of liquid from the pot and slowly whisk into the egg-lemon mix. Pour this over the *yiouvarlakia* and shake the pot so that the sauce covers them.

Serve immediately with some of the sauce.

Following pages: *Kastellorizo with Turkey in the distance.*

Saganaki

Fried cheese

Saganaki is the thin, aluminium, two-handled frying pan used to cook and serve this dish. Most of the hard Greek cheeses can be used, although the favourites are the salty *kefalotiri*, *kasseri* and Cypriot *halloumi* (which can be grilled).

SERVES 4-6
225 g/8 oz *kefalotiri* or *haloumi*
30 ml/2 tbsp flour
30 ml/2 tbsp olive oil
1 lemon, quartered
15 ml/1 tbsp dried oregano (optional)

Cut the cheese into 1 cm/½ inch thick slices and dust with flour. Heat the oil in the *saganaki* or alternative frying pan and when it is very hot, fry the cheese for 2 minutes on each side until golden brown. Serve immediately, with a squeeze of lemon juice and oregano sprinkled on top.

When frying, make sure the slices are kept apart, otherwise they tend to stick together. That is why one large slice is fried in a *saganaki* pan in the *ouzerie* and served individually at the table.

Glossary

Achinous Sea urchins
Achladia Pears
Agrafa Cheese similar to Gruyere
Alevri Flour
Ameletita Offal
Amigthala Almonds
Anari Goat's cheese similar to Gorgonzola
Anginares Artichokes
Angouri Cucumber
Anitho Dill
Anthotyri Goat's cheese from Crete
Arakas Peas
Arnaki Lamb
Bahari All spice
Bamies Okra/Ladies fingers
Bobota Corn bread
Bourekakia Small filo pastries
Briki Traditional metal or copper utensil
Dafni Bay leaves
Dendrolivano Rosemary
Diosmo Mint
Diples Fried knot and bow shaped pastries served with honey and cinnamon
Exochiko Method of baking marinated lamb with cheese in paper
Faskomoilo Sage tea
Fide Vermicelli noodles used in soups
Fragosika Prickly pears
Friganies Rusks
Foulia Egyptian 'ful medames' beans
Gala Milk
Galopoulo Turkey
Garifalo Cloves
Gemista Stuffed vegetable dishes
Glossa Tongue, also the word for flat fish like sole/flounder

Hamomili Chamomile
Hilopittes Egg-noodles
Hourmades Dates
Kafe Coffee; *sketos* without sugar, *me oligi* with a little sugar, *metrio* medium sweet, *glikes vrastos* sweet
Kaimaki Froth on a Turkish coffee, also a special ice-cream
Kalamboki Sweet-corn
Kanella Cinnamon
Kapamas Spicy cooking method for stewed chicken and lamb dishes that uses hot peppers, cloves and cinnamon
Karavides Crayfish
Karpouzi Water-melon
Karvouna Charcoal grilling
Kokkinisto Method of cooking chicken and beef with tomato to give it a red (*kokkino*) colour
Kolios Mackerel
Kounoupidi Cauliflower
Krasato Method of cooking in wine
Kremmidia Onions
Kymino Cumin
Ladocarto Method of baking parcels of lamb or beef stew in paper
Ladolemono Oil and lemon dressing
Ladorigani Method of cooking meat stews with oregano and olive oil
Lemonato Method of cooking meat stews with lemon and olive oil
Loukoumades Fried ball-shaped doughnuts
Maidano Parsley
Makaronia General name for all pasta
Manitaria Mushrooms
Maratho Wild fennel
Marinata Method of marinating and cooking meat and fish

Mavromatika Black-eyed beans
Meli Honey
Melitzanes Aubergines/eggplants
Melomakarona Cakes with honey
Midia Mussels
Milo Apple
Mousmoula Loquats
Nerantzia Bitter orange preserve
Oktapodi Octopus
Paidakia Lamb chops sold by weight in restaurants
Patates Potatoes
Patsaria Beetroot; often served with *scordalia* garlic sauce
Peponi Melon
Pestrofa Trout
Piaz fasolia Haricot bean salad with chopped onion, tomato, parsley and oil
Piperies Peppers
Pittes Pies made with filo pastry
Plaki Rich style of baking fish and beans
Pligouri Cracked wheat
Portokalia Oranges
Prassa Leeks
Psito Method of roasting meat
Psomi Bread
Rapanakia Radishes
Ravani Semolina cake
Renges Smoked or salted herrings
Revithia Chick-peas
Rigani Oregano
Rizi Rice
Rodia Pomegranates
Saganaki Fried cheese
Salmi Method of cooking game; stewed with red wine, celery, carrot and herbs
Saltses Sauces

Selinorizo Celeriac; usually stewed with pork
Sikoti Liver
Skaras another name for grilling
Skordo Garlic; *skordato* method of cooking meat with garlic
Smyrneika Method of cooking in Smyrna style
Soupia Cuttlefish
Spetsiotiko Method of baking fish with garlic, parsley and wine
Stafides Raisins
Stifado Stew
Syka Figs
Tarama Fish roe, *taramasalata* or *taramakeftedes*
Tiganites Fried
Toursi Pickles
Trachana Crushed wheat and dried sheep's milk
Tsai Tea, *tsai vourno* mountain herbal tea
Tyri Cheese
Tzatziki Yoghurt, cucumber, garlic, and mint dip
Verikoka Apricot
Vissino/Vissinada Cherry, cherry cordial
Votana Wild herbs
Voutiro Butter
Vrasto Boiled
Vrouves Mustard greens/charlock
Xydi Vinegar
Yiachni Method of stewing with tomatoes and onions of Turkish origin
Yaourti Yoghurt
Youvetsi Takes its name from the earthenware casserole dish used to bake meat and pasta dishes
Zachari Sugar

Index

Page numbers in *italics* denote illustrations

A
Aetolikon, *121*
Aetopetra, 113
Albania, 102
Alexandroupolis, 100
Ano Meria, 97
Amficlea, 92, 95
Ancient Greeks, 40, 41
Anidro, 52, 53
Antikeros, 51
Arachova, 95
Arki, 49, *50*, *51*

C
caique, the, 47-48
Chania market, Crete, 70, *73*
Chios, 56
Christmas, 23
Corfu, 64
Crete, 7, 64-79
Cyclades, 38

D
Delphi, 95

E
Easter celebrations, 23, 59
Edirne, 100
Epirus, 92, 107, 111, *114*, 121
Eptalofos, 95

F
Farmakonisi, 50
Florina, 106, 107

G
Galaxidi, 125
Gamila, Epirus, *87*
Gavros, *102*

H
Halkidiki, *92*
Hecate, 40
Herodotus, 13

I
Ioannina, 109, *117*, 117, 119, 121
Iraklion, Crete, *79*, 79

J
Jason and the Argonauts, 95

K
Kalymnos, 53
Kamena Vourla, *89*, 89
Kas, *56*, 64
Kastellorizo, *56*, 58-64, *60*, *64*
Kastoria, *89*, 104, 106, *107*, 107
Kavala, 101
Keros, 51
Koufonissia, 51, *52*, 52
Kamena Vourla, 89

L
Lake Kastoria, 89
Lake Pamvotis, *119*
Lamia, 92
Lesbos, (see Mitilini)

M
Macedonia, 92
Mani, 7
Manzion, *109*, 111
Megali Prespa, *104*
Megalo Papingo, 113
Megisti, (see Kastellorizo)
Messolonghi, *121*, 121
Metsovo, 109, *114*, 114
Mikri Prespa, *104*, 104
Mikro Papingo, 113
Milies, 97, *100*

Mytilini, 37, 54, 56
Mount Arachinthos, 123
Mount Olympus, 87
Mount Parnassus, 92
Mount Pelion, 95
Mykonos, 30
Mytilini, 7

O
olive harvesting, 70
Omonia Square, Athens, *132*
Ottoman Empire, 7, 56, 64, 117, 118

P
Paleopolis, 100
Parnassus, 95
Pelion, 92, *95*, 97
Peloponnese, the, 22
Piraeus, *139*, *140*, 140
Plaka, Athens, 137, *143*
Plato, 40
Pomaki, 99
Prasses, *74*
Prespa Lakes, 102
Psarades, *104*

R
Rethymnon, Crete, 77, 79

Rhodes, 7
Roman Empire, 7, 40, 56
Roumeli, 92

S
Samaria Gorge, Crete, 64
Samothrace, 100
Santorini, 9, 30, *47*
Sappho, 54

Syros, 54

T
Theophilos, 95
Therissos, Crete, *74*, 74
Thessaloniki, 101, 102
Theophilos, 56, 95
Thrace, 22, 92, 99, 100, 101
Tilos, *47*, 56

tourism, 23, 28
Trikeri, 95
Tsarouchis, 97
Turkey, 22

V
Venetian rule, 64
Visitza, 99

W
wine-making, *17*

X
Xanthi, 101

Z
Zagoria, 113
Zagorochorio, *92*